THE FREEDOM SUMMER ★MURDERS★

DON MITCHELL

SCHOLASTIC PRESS | NEW YORK

Photographs ©: AP Images: 141 (Anonymous), 102, 103 (Bettmann), 164
(Charles Smith), v, 156 (Danny Johnston), i *top center*, 15 *center*, 15 *bottom*,
31 (FBI), 137 (HWC), 23 (JAB), 145 (Jack Thornell), vi *top left*, 98 (JEB),
132 (John Lindsay), 126, 171 (Kyle Carter), 177 (Lynda Edwards), 168, 176
(Rogelio V. Solis), 20 (Strat Douthat), 8, 10, 124, 152; Archives of the Andrew
Goodman Foundation: jacket back *top right*, *bottom* iii, 37, 39, 40, 45, 52
top, 52 *bottom*, 56, 58, 59, 60, 150, 178; Author's Collection: *top* iii, 12;
Bedrich Grunzweig Photo Archive/© Bedrich Grunzweig, 1961: 46; Corbis
Images: jacket front, jacket back *top left*, i *top left*, i *top right*, 15 *top*, 28,
30, 32, 33 *top*, 33 *bottom*, 34, 67, 78, 95, 129, 131, 146 (Bettmann), 4
(Bob Adelman), 174 *bottom* (Kyle Carter), jacket back *bottom*, 105 *top*,
105 *bottom*, 107 (Steve Schapiro), 7, 122; Getty Images: 139 (Bill Ray),
jacket back flap (Danny Johnston), 197 (Encyclopaedia Britannica), 170, 174
top, 182 (Marianne Todd), 172 (Pool), jacket front flap, 135 (Robert Abbott
Sengstacke); Magnum Photos/Danny Lyon: 96; Mississippi Department of
Archives and History, Courtesy of the Archives and Records Services Division:
113, 114; Newseum/Ted Polumbaum: 109; Patti Miller/Keeping History Alive:
24, 85; Redux/Keith Meyers/*The New York Times*: 73; The Image Works:
128 (George Ballis), jacket back *center*, vi *top right*, 2, 6, 25 (Matt Herron).

Library of Congress Cataloging-in-Publication Data Available

ISBN 978-0-545-47725-3

10 9 8 7 6 5 4 3 2 1   14 15 16 17 18/0

Printed in the U.S.A.   23
First edition, May 2014

Book design by Jeannine Riske
Photo research by Marybeth Kavanagh

For Grace, who knows what it means to take a risk for freedom

CONTENTS

THIS MEMORIAL IS PRAYERFULLY
AND PROUDLY DEDICATED
TO THE MEMORY OF

JAMES CHANEY
ANDREW GOODMAN
MICHAEL SCHWERNER

WHO GAVE THEIR LIVES IN THE
STRUGGLE TO OBTAIN HUMAN
RIGHTS FOR ALL PEOPLE.

"WE SHALL NOT BE MOVED"

Chorus:
We shall not, we shall not be moved,
We shall not, we shall not be moved;
Just like a tree that's standing by the water,
We shall not be moved.

We're fighting for our freedom, we shall not be moved,
We're fighting for our freedom, we shall not be moved;
Just like a tree that's standing by the water,
We shall not be moved.

Chorus

We must stand and fight together, we shall not be moved,
We must stand and fight together, we shall not be moved;
Just like a tree that's standing by the water,
We shall not be moved.

Chorus

PROLOGUE

Be ashamed to die until you have won some victory for humanity.

  — Horace Mann, Antioch College commencement address, Yellow Springs, Ohio, 1859

In June 1964, Willie Peacock, a member of the civil rights organization the Student Nonviolent Coordinating Committee (SNCC), was arrested, along with several black colleagues, on a trumped-up traffic charge outside Columbus, Mississippi. He was describing his treatment from the police officers in the county jail to a group of civil rights volunteers:

"Nigger, do you believe I'd just as soon kill you as look at you?"

"Yes," Willie responded to the police officer. But he wasn't fast enough. *Whack!* Willie was struck with the officer's left hand.

Willie looked out at the sea of mostly white college students who had come to this safe, idyllic school nestled in the rolling farmlands of southwestern Ohio. He was giving them a firsthand account of what life was like in the South. And he unnerved his audience when Willie's colleague occasionally

Willie Peacock *(front row, third from left)* attended a rally on the steps of the Hinds County Courthouse in Jackson, Mississippi, in October 1963.

rubbed his aching jaw where his teeth were still loose from the beating he took in that Mississippi jail just a few weeks before. Willie and his friends were speaking to the Freedom Summer volunteers who were training here in Oxford in preparation to live in Mississippi for the summer and register blacks to vote.

Willie warned his idealistic young listeners: "When you go down those cold stairs at the police station, you don't know if you're going to come back or not. You don't know if you can take those licks without fighting back, because you might decide to fight back. It all depends on how you want to die."

INTRODUCTION

To be born black and to live in Mississippi was to say that your life wasn't worth much.

— Myrlie Evers, wife of slain civil rights leader Medgar Evers

Blacks in the South were second-class citizens at best. Mississippi, like other southern states, operated under a policy of segregation, which meant keeping the white and black races separate. Blacks had different — and usually inferior — restaurants, restrooms, drinking fountains, waiting rooms, schools, hospitals, and housing. It was understood that blacks must be deferential to whites in virtually every interaction. If you were black and walking on the public sidewalk and white people approached, you had to step down into the street and let the white people use the sidewalk. And public transportation? If you were black, your place was at the back of the bus. And if the bus was crowded and a white passenger needed a seat, you better stand and give up that seat or it could mean jail, or a beating.

In its 1896 ruling in *Plessy v. Ferguson*, the US Supreme Court validated racial segregation in Mississippi and

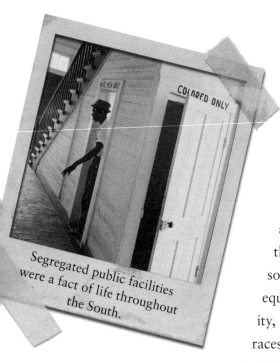
Segregated public facilities were a fact of life throughout the South.

elsewhere when it ruled that states could require separate facilities (e.g., transportation, schools, restaurants) for blacks and whites as long as they were equal — the so-called "separate but equal" doctrine. But in reality, while facilities for the races were frequently separate, they were seldom equal. The 1954 ruling in the case of *Brown v. Board of Education* overturned "separate but equal." Segregation in public schools was prohibited and states were required to integrate immediately.

But white officials in Mississippi dug in and refused to desegregate their schools. The white supremacists were determined to detect and destroy any effort to end segregation.

A July 1954 meeting of concerned whites in Indianola, Mississippi, led to the creation of the first Citizens' Council. By October 1954, the council claimed to have more than twenty-five thousand members. The council was dedicated to preserving Mississippi's social order of white dominance and the organized resistance to any federal government efforts in support of integration. Its membership was comprised of white citizens, many of whom were businessmen who believed that segregation could be preserved through legal, nonviolent means. The council simply relied on the use of threats, coercion, and economic retaliation against those who sought to change the status quo.

The most effective way for Mississippi's white elites to deprive blacks of their voice in government was to deny them the right to vote. Individuals who tried to register blacks to vote, or encourage others to do so, could find themselves out of a job and labeled as virtually unemployable. Local banks could refuse to extend them credit, loans, or home mortgages. The council would take out advertisements in newspapers and list the names and addresses of individuals who were, or were suspected of being, civil rights activists. The white community would react quickly to these postings. Insurance policies could be canceled. Boycotts were arranged against merchants who were sympathetic to the civil rights movement.

The government of Mississippi felt so strongly about the need to protect segregation, it created its own spy agency to deal with the threat of integration. By an act of the Mississippi legislature, the Mississippi State Sovereignty Commission was created on March 29, 1956. The new organization was granted extensive investigatory powers. Anyone, black or white, who expressed support for integration, was involved in civil rights, or even had suspect political affiliations was a fitting target for commission investigators. The Sovereignty Commission exercised far-reaching authority on the people of Mississippi. It banned books, censored films, and closely

NOTICE

Applications for Registration must be completely filled out without any assistance or suggestions of any person or memorandum.

After 10 days applicants names and addresses are published for two consecutive weeks in the newspaper. They cannot be ruled on until 14 days after the second publication. Therefore it can take as long as 33 days before we can give you an answer as to your application being accepted or rejected.

Your indulgence is appreciated.
The Registrar

In January 1964, at a courthouse in Mississippi, black applicants attempt to register to vote. The wall sign warns of the public exposure applicants will experience in order to intimidate black citizens.

examined school curriculums. It even censored national radio broadcasts and television programs.

Mississippi's white racists fought ferociously to maintain their supremacy, and many blacks were harassed, arrested, beaten, and even murdered. For many years before the 1964 Freedom Summer, Mississippi held a special place of terror for America's black population. Indeed, blacks were victimized by violence in Mississippi perhaps more than anywhere else in the United States. And lynching, in which mobs took the law into their own hands, was the ultimate penalty. Lynchings often, but not always, involved hanging a person from the neck until they died. While available records likely underestimate the scope of the practice, during the period from 1889 to 1945, more lynchings were held in Mississippi than any other state. Most of the victims were young black men who were suspected of assaulting a white person or who in some way challenged the system of segregation.

Many whites joined the Ku Klux Klan — or the KKK, as it was commonly known. The KKK was established in 1867 following the Civil War. The Klansmen hid behind masked costumes, which were intended to conceal their identities, as well as to strike fear into their victims. Local authorities were seldom willing to stop them. The Klan and similar groups didn't hesitate to use threats, violence, and lynching to establish and maintain white supremacy.

This 1872 print depicts members of the Ku Klux Klan, or KKK, as it was commonly known.

On the evening of May 7, 1955, Reverend George W. Lee, who had recently spoken at a voter registration rally, was driving along a street in Belzoni, Mississippi, when a car following him sped up and pulled alongside him. Someone in the car fired several shots at Lee, killing him. No one was ever arrested for the murder. An even bolder murder was committed on August 13, 1955, on a busy Saturday afternoon on the courthouse lawn in the Mississippi town of Brookhaven. The victim was Lamar Smith, a sixty-three-year-old local farmer who was organizing blacks to vote. Despite numerous witnesses, no one would admit to seeing a white man shoot a black man, and no one was ever brought to justice for the murder.

A significant milestone in the battle for equality occurred in Mississippi when a determined young veteran of the US Air Force named James Meredith decided he wanted to be the first black to attend the University of Mississippi — Ole Miss — in Oxford in the fall of 1962. The university was an almost sacred part of Mississippi tradition, and therefore a place where blacks were

John Doar (left rear) and federal marshals escort James Meredith (right rear) on his first day.

not welcome. While federal marshals protected Meredith in a campus dormitory, a riot broke out, resulting in the death of a local bystander and a French reporter. President John F. Kennedy addressed the nation, called for calm, and ultimately had to send federal forces to Oxford to break up the riot. James Meredith went on to graduate from Ole Miss.

The triumph of integration at Ole Miss only increased white hostility in the state. In early June 1963, a group of black civil rights activists were taking a Greyhound bus back to Mississippi after a one-week course on citizenship that was being sponsored by the civil rights organization the Southern Christian Leadership Conference (SCLC) in Charleston, South Carolina. The group had tried to integrate the restaurant and lunch counter at the Winona bus station. They were arrested, and the police beat several members of the group, including Fannie Lou Hamer. The Justice Department charged the local sheriff and the other men with conspiracy to deprive the prisoners of their civil rights. Ultimately, a federal jury comprised of local white men in Oxford, Mississippi, found the accused not guilty.

On June 11, 1963, just days after Fannie Lou Hamer's savage beating in Winona, Medgar Evers, the state field secretary for the Mississippi National Association for the Advancement of Colored People (NAACP), was assassinated in front of his home in Jackson, Mississippi. At Evers's funeral, police and demonstrators clashed, and a riot was narrowly averted. A member of the white Citizens' Council

Medgar Evers, field secretary for the Mississippi NAACP

from Greenwood, Mississippi, Byron De La Beckwith, was arrested as a suspect in the murder. Despite overwhelming evidence, De La Beckwith went free after two trials ended in a hung jury.

In the fall of 1963, the Council of Federated Organizations (COFO), an umbrella organization of civil rights groups operating in Mississippi, created the "Freedom Ballot for Governor" initiative. Civil rights activists then worked on a massive statewide "freedom vote" campaign for the general election. On Election Day, more than eighty-three thousand freedom votes were cast in churches, stores, and other gathering places for the black community. The freedom vote expanded the level of civil rights efforts throughout the state, educated blacks about voter registration and voting, and created a political organization.

Mississippi's civil rights leaders considered their next steps, focusing on grassroots work in the state and bringing in people from out of state to generate publicity and financial assistance. Gradually, a consensus was built on the need for a major voter registration effort in the summer of 1964. The initiative became known as Freedom Summer.

The growing determination of Mississippi's civil rights activists was matched by the state's white racists who thought that they needed to take a harder stance against them. The Citizens' Council had been a leading force over the past decade to intimidate and keep blacks "in line," primarily through economic retribution. However, other whites thought this wasn't enough, and they became increasingly frustrated, angry — and more inclined to use violence. The Klan offered a natural outlet.

In December 1963, Klansmen in Mississippi formed the White Knights of the Ku Klux Klan, which became dominant in the state and the most violent Klan faction. The Imperial Wizard, or leader, of the White Knights was a forty-year-old businessman and World War II veteran named Sam Bowers, whose stated objective was the destruction of the civil rights movement in Mississippi. By the middle of 1964, approximately five thousand white Mississippians had joined the Ku Klux Klan. And they quickly made their presence known. There were cross burnings throughout the state. Black homes, businesses, and churches were bombed, and individuals were targeted for beatings and shootings. Some Mississippi whites were concerned about this spike in violence, as they feared that it could lead to greater sympathy for the civil rights movement and increase momentum for the passage of federal civil rights legislation. They had little sympathy for the

This 1964 SNCC pamphlet for the Mississippi Summer Project solicits volunteers.

victims of Klan violence and made hardly any effort to apprehend and bring to justice those responsible.

As the violence raged on in Mississippi, several hundred people descended on the Western College for Women in Oxford, Ohio, in June 1964 to prepare for their role in Freedom Summer. They were mostly young white volunteers filled with good intentions. Some left in the face of warnings about the grim realities awaiting them in Mississippi. But most of the volunteers stayed.

The volunteers were divided into two groups: those who would travel from house to house in Mississippi's black communities, persuading people to take a risk and register to vote, and those who would be teaching at the freedom schools that were to be established throughout the state. The teachers would be educating Mississippi blacks — both young and old — about civics and black history, among other subjects, for the summer.

Another group also converged on the campus. They were the black, battle-hardened veterans of the civil rights struggle in Mississippi. Like Willie Peacock, they had few, if any, illusions about what was in store for the white volunteers. And they were determined to give their summer guests a crash course in what to expect. They knew their training could help save the lives of the student volunteers. Most of the Mississippi veterans were members of SNCC, and they were determined to convert these idealists into realists and train them in the skills to succeed and to survive.

The volunteers also heard from John Doar, the Justice Department's assistant attorney general in the civil rights division. Doar was highly respected as a friend of the civil rights movement. When asked what the Justice Department would do to assist Freedom Summer volunteers, he was blunt. "Nothing. There is no federal police force. The responsibility for protection is that of the local police." And few people in the group had any illusions that they would receive assistance from Mississippi's local police. Jess Brown, one of only a handful of black lawyers in Mississippi, bluntly explained the facts of life to the assembled volunteers. He warned the young people that where they were going, people would classify them into two groups: "niggers and nigger lovers. And they're tougher on nigger lovers."

This was the environment that the young Freedom Summer volunteers boldly walked into during the summer of 1964. And this is the story of three young men who placed their faith in nonviolence in the service of civil rights and social justice:

James Chaney, a twenty-one-year-old black man and a native of Mississippi who wanted a better life for his family and his people;

Andrew Goodman, a twenty-year-old white college student from New York who believed it was important to act on his beliefs and fight against injustice; and

Michael Schwerner, a married twenty-four-year-old white social worker and civil rights organizer from New York who was committed to working toward an integrated society.

On June 21, 1964, these three young men were brutally murdered by the Ku Klux Klan, with the complicity of the local police, for trying to help blacks as part of the 1964 Freedom Summer voter registration effort in Mississippi. Their disappearance and the eventual discovery of their bodies caused a national uproar and was one of the most significant events of the American civil rights movement. The murder of the three civil rights workers marked the height of armed resistance to racial equality in Mississippi — arguably the state most resistant to such change at the time.

This is the story of idealistic, courageous young people who wanted to change the world for the better. It is the story of how their sacrifice helped change their country for the better. It is a story of black and white. And ultimately, it is the story of our nation's endless struggle to close the gap between what is and what ought to be.

James Chaney

Andrew Goodman

Michael Schwerner

CHAPTER 1
A PLANNED, DELIBERATE MURDER

When historians weigh the sixth decade of the twentieth century in the United States, they will call this murder one of the revealing acts of the decade. It was a planned, deliberate murder to try to prevent racial change; and it was committed by men who called themselves Christians and thought they were doing right.

— William Bradford Huie

"Lord, don't let them kill my husband."

Beatrice Cole pleaded for the life of her husband, Roosevelt "Bud" Cole. It was Tuesday evening, June 16, 1964. She and her husband were trying to get home after attending a meeting at the Mount Zion Methodist Church in Longdale, Mississippi. Longdale was an all-black community in rural Neshoba County, about eight miles from Philadelphia, Mississippi, and thirty-five miles from Meridian. But the couple got no farther than the entrance to the churchyard. A white man with two pistols in his holsters stepped in front of them. Along the nearby roadside, twenty-five to thirty white men appeared along a ditch with rifles at the ready. In the face of hostile questioning, Bud denied that the church meeting had anything to do with voter registration or civil rights. Enraged by his denials, the white men began beating Bud Cole.

"We are innocent as lambs," Beatrice continued. "Never have harmed nobody. Tried to treat everybody right." As the men continued to kick her husband, she asked to be allowed to pray.

"If you think prayer will do you any good, you'd better pray," the white leader replied.

"It's too late to pray now," another white man added.

"It's never too late to pray," replied Beatrice.

"Pray then."

Beatrice fell to her knees in the sandy ruts of the road and raised her hands toward the moonlit sky, with her palms pressed tightly together. "Father, I stretch my hands to thee. No other help I know. If thou withdraw thyself from me, Lord, whither shall I go? Lord, will you spare my husband's life? Please don't let them kill my husband." Beatrice later recalled that her prayer "struck the hearts of those men. The Lord was there, because then the man said, 'Let her alone,' and he looked kind of sick about it." With that, the white men threw Bud Cole into the weeds. The white man told the other vigilantes, "Load up." And they left.

Bud Cole was still alive. Beatrice went to her battered husband and helped him to their car as the attackers got in their vehicles and drove out onto the Longdale road. The Coles got to their house a quarter mile down the dirt road from the church. Bud wouldn't allow his wife to call the doctor that night because he was afraid white men might still be lurking about. Others in the community were also harassed that evening.

Georgia Rush and her twenty-four-year-old son, John Thomas "J.T." Rush Jr., also attended the meeting at Mount Zion that night. As they were leaving, they were stopped by a group of about fifteen to twenty white men. J.T. was dragged out of his pickup truck. "At this point they asked us what kind of a meeting we had been holding and where were the white people who were supposed to be at the meeting," he recalled. J.T. was then ordered to drive his truck into a ditch, was told to get out, and was beaten. His mother told the Federal Bureau of Investigation (FBI), "They pulled J.T. from the car and struck him across the shoulders and neck. They also struck me across the face and shoulders with some heavy object." Then, mother and son drove back home. Georgia's eighteen-year-old daughter, Jewel, recalled her mother coming into the house, "and she's all bloody and crying, and my brother has been beat about the head, and he's got blood on him." Jewel's mother refused to go see a doctor, and the family was terrified that night "that somebody would shoot in the house, or somebody would set the house on fire or burn some crosses in our yard." They sat up and kept the house lights off. The family wasn't bothered anymore that evening.

Shortly before 1:00 a.m. that same night, nearby residents noticed a glow in the sky as the sixty-five-year-old Mount Zion Methodist Church burned to the ground. All that was left was the church's bell. Beatrice had supported the church being used as a freedom school for that summer, but

Bud had opposed it, fearing it would only bring trouble to their community. Nevertheless, his wife never regretted it. Beatrice would later say that "[i]f they're going to kill you, you might as well die for something. We're going to have to struggle a good bit more before day breaks."

Just a few weeks earlier, on Memorial Day, Mickey Schwerner had spoken at Mount Zion, urging the black congregation to take an important step toward equality by supporting the voter registration effort. He asked the congregants to allow the church to be used as a freedom school during Freedom Summer that was rapidly approaching. "You have been slaves too long," he told them. "We can help you help yourselves. . . . Meet us here, and we'll train you so you can qualify to vote." James Chaney, who had accompanied Mickey, spoke to the congregation after Mickey. The earnest young civil rights workers won over most of the congregation, and it was agreed there would be a freedom school there that summer.

Mickey was nowhere near Neshoba County the night the church was destroyed. He; his wife, Rita; James; and others had already departed Meridian and traveled to Oxford, Ohio, to help train volunteers for Freedom Summer. Mickey heard about the church burning the next day, and he was anxious to go there and be with the people who had paid such a heavy price for doing what he had asked of them.

On Friday evening, June 19, Freedom Summer volunteers and staff gathered for a final session of group singing. The first session of training was ending, and Mickey and

IS MEMORIAL IS PRAYERFULLY
AND PROUDLY DEDICATED
TO THE MEMORY OF

JAMES CHANEY
ANDREW GOODMAN
MICHAEL SCHWERNER

HO GAVE THEIR LIVES IN THE
TRUGGLE TO OBTAIN HUMAN

Beatrice and Roosevelt "Bud" Cole next to the memorial for
the three civil rights workers in front of the rebuilt Mount
Zion Methodist Church in January 1989.

James were planning on pulling out of the Oxford campus with a small group of volunteers at 3:00 a.m. the next morning in order to get to Meridian before the sun went down Saturday night. Rita had been asked to stay on in Oxford for the next week to help with training, and she had reluctantly agreed.

Rita recalled Mickey's departure in the wee hours of that Saturday morning. "There was nothing very special about it. Somebody knocked on the door and said it was time to go. He was dressed in three or four minutes — I think he had on blue jeans — and then he came over to the bed and said, 'I'm leaving now.' It was all settled, so he kissed me good-bye and left and I didn't go down to the car. I rolled over and went back to sleep." That was the last time Rita saw Mickey.

One of the volunteers they were taking to Mississippi was Andy Goodman. Andy had arrived in Oxford on the evening of Saturday, June 13, for the first week of Freedom Summer training. Before long, Andy met the Schwerners and "all of us were delighted with him," recalled Rita. "He was such a fine, intelligent, unassuming young man. He and I had much to talk about because he was a student at my alma mater, Queens College." Impressed with his fellow New Yorker, Mickey invited Andy to come and work with him in Meridian. Despite the burning of the church in Longdale, Mickey was determined to go ahead with plans for the freedom school there, but he needed someone with the skills to take on that increasingly challenging assignment. On Friday night,

June 19, Andy telephoned his mother to tell her that he would be working with Mickey and Rita Schwerner.

There were eight people in the station wagon when they left Oxford, two of whom were women. Except for James, all the occupants were white. When they drove through Birmingham, Alabama, a group of white teenagers passed them on the road and shouted, "Nigger lovers!" After this incident, the group changed their seating arrangement to make sure that James wasn't sitting next to any of the white women.

When they arrived in Meridian, the other students were placed with the black families who had agreed to house them. Because Andy had not been originally assigned to Meridian for the summer, it was agreed that he would stay with Mickey at the Schwerners' apartment until he could find accommodations. The three men then drove to James Chaney's home, where Mickey and Rita had enjoyed a great deal of hospitality during their stay in Meridian. After visiting with the Chaneys, the three went to see an old horror movie at a black theater in downtown Meridian. After dropping Andy and Mickey off at the Schwerners' apartment, James returned home and stayed up to talk to his mother, Fannie Lee, about his experience in Oxford and the Freedom Summer project. Fannie Lee recalled, "It was one of the best times we ever had, quiet and easylike. As James went to bed, he said, 'Mom, cook up lots of food tomorrow. All the students are coming over.' He kissed me, and that was the last time I ever saw him."

The three young civil rights workers woke up on Sunday, June 21, 1964. It was Father's Day. And it was to be the longest day of the year, the day of the summer solstice.

Mickey and Andy had breakfast at a café across the street from the community center in Meridian. They came to the center first, followed by James. The other workers gathered at the center at around 8:30 a.m., excited with the anticipation of meeting the new people who were going to help for the summer. Sue Brown, who was in charge of the center in Rita's absence, recalled that morning: "Mickey was full of ideas and enthusiasms, but the main thing on his mind was Longdale. He knew several of the Longdale people had been beaten up, and he wanted to visit them. He wanted the Longdale people to meet Andy, and he wanted to make plans to hold the freedom school up there on the grounds of the burned church."

Was it necessary for Mickey to go to Longdale just as Freedom Summer was beginning, when white paranoia and antipathy toward the "outside agitators" was likely going to be at a high point? Two whites traveling with a black would be

Sue Brown *(right)* at the COFO office in Meridian, in 1964.

conspicuous on such a day in Neshoba County, which was particularly hostile to civil rights workers. Wouldn't it have been safer to wait and visit another time?

Rita believed the trip to Longdale was essential. "They had to go back and see those people," she said. "You don't abandon people who have put themselves at risk." Roscoe Jones, a teenage civil rights worker at the Meridian community center, believed that Mickey's strong loyalty to the people he had asked to take a risk for his civil rights initiatives could be exploited by those who wanted to harm Mickey. The church burning was a death trap. "The Klan knew that

Freedom Summer volunteers read to children
at the Meridian community center.

the only way they could get him up there [in Neshoba County] was to burn that church down. And Goatee [the Klan's nickname for Mickey] would come running, because he was a Good Samaritan. It worked. And he went up there."

Sue Brown noted that "[o]urs wasn't a waiting operation. Our word was *now*. Freedom *now*. Mickey was serious. He was concerned. He knew that going to Longdale was

A recruiting poster for the White Knights
of Mississippi KKK

dangerous. But those people up there had taken risks and suffered, and he thought he ought to go. He *wanted* to go. He took some precautions. Three or four other people asked to go with him, but he narrowed them down to Jim and Andy. About nine thirty or close to ten he sat down with me and went over the travel plan. He said he had a few things to do in Meridian, like getting his hair cut and the car serviced, but that he expected to be in Longdale by noon, he'd spend about three hours up there, and he'd be back at the center at four p.m."

Security was important for civil rights workers in Mississippi. When people were on the road, it was important to check in with their home base by a certain time. If they didn't call in on time, the home office would begin calling local police stations and deploy other resources to hunt down the travelers, and hopefully prevent something serious from happening. Knowing how dangerous the trip to Longdale would be that morning, Sue asked him: "If you're not back at four, what time do I start calling?" Mickey responded, "At four thirty. But we'll be back by four."

Mickey and Andy received a haircut that morning from David Sims, a barber who sometimes helped in local civil rights work and who grew up next door to the Chaney family. Years later, he remembered Mickey Schwerner fondly: "Mickey was a kid; he was a loving fellow. He didn't believe anybody would hurt a fly, especially not those white folks down south." Sims encountered Andy only that one time. "I didn't know him, but I was probably the last one to have my hands on his head."

Later, on June 21, Ernest Kirkland, a Longdale resident, brought Mickey, James, and Andy by the Rushes' house to see Georgia and talk about the beating at the church. Everyone was gone when they arrived except for one of Jewel's brothers. When they came home, Jewel recalled that her brother told their mother, " 'There was some guys here looking for you.' She said, 'Who was it?' He said, 'I don't know, there was three guys and Ernest wanted to talk to you about the beating.' My mother went, 'Oh Lord.' So we still didn't know who they were. About ten o'clock when the news come on in Meridian, everybody used to sit up and watch the Sunday news. Here, the pictures pop up on the screen that they were missing. And that's when my brother that was home said, 'That's the guys that came by here to see you.' And my mother said, 'Oh my Lord, something has happened to them. Somebody has killed them.' "

After making their visits to other people in the local community, the three men took off for Meridian at around 2:00 p.m., with James at the wheel. While still in Neshoba County, Deputy Sheriff Cecil Price pulled over the vehicle. He arrested James on a trumped-up charge of speeding, and the two white men were held for "investigation." Price brought them to the jail in Philadelphia around 4:00 p.m., where they were locked up and not allowed to make a phone call. They would spend about six hours in the jail while Deputy Sheriff Price allegedly had to find a magistrate to address Chaney's speeding charge. But prosecutors would later argue that this was time necessary for Price to tip off the Ku Klux Klan to formulate

Deputy Sheriff Cecil Price

and execute a plan to murder Goatee and his friends.

Mickey had said they'd be back in Meridian by 4:00 p.m., and when the three hadn't returned by then, the community center staff began implementing emergency procedures. They telephoned civil rights program offices throughout the state as well as police stations throughout the area. The COFO offices called the Neshoba County jail at 5:30 p.m., and whoever answered the phone denied having seen the three men. At that point, their fates were sealed. The fact that the three men were currently residing in their tiny jail was information to be shared only with the Ku Klux Klan. FBI and Department of Justice officials were also notified of the disappearance but would do nothing absent evidence of a violation of federal law.

When Mickey, James, and Andy didn't return to Meridian that Sunday afternoon, Roscoe Jones believed that the worst had happened. When Roscoe went home that night, he told his grandmother, " 'Mickey and them is missing. They're dead.' And at that time they were still alive; probably about an hour later they were dead. I didn't talk to anybody about it. I blocked it out of my mind. I knew they was dead."

Several members of the lynch party would later cooperate with federal authorities and provide an account of what happened that night. One of the witnesses was Klansman James Jordan. He described the role played by Preacher Edgar Ray Killen in planning and organizing the murders. Killen met with Klansmen at Meridian's Longhorn Drive-in, and later at Akin's Mobile Homes, to recruit volunteers for the operation. According to Jordan, Killen said that "they had three civil rights workers in jail in Philadelphia and that they needed their 'asses tore up.' Killen said that it had to be done in a hurry since they were being held on a minor charge. He further said that they would need four or five men from Lauderdale County to go and that there would be several from Neshoba County."

Another participant in the evening's events was Klansman Horace Doyle Barnette. Barnette stated that when he and other Klansmen arrived in Philadelphia around 9:30 p.m., they met Killen, who got into Barnette's car and told him to park in a location where they could wait until the three young men would be released from the jail. Killen told Barnette that "we have a place to bury them and a man to run the dozer to cover them up." Barnette stated that this was "the first time I realized that the three civil rights workers were to be killed."

At 10:00 p.m., Deputy Sheriff Price returned to the jail to release the three men, with James paying the twenty-dollar

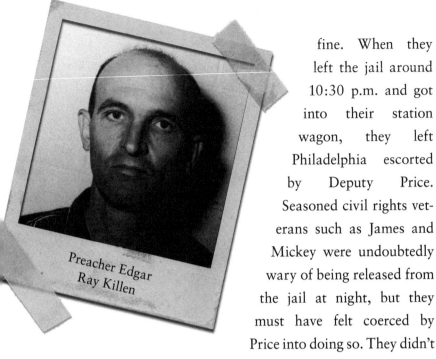

Preacher Edgar Ray Killen

fine. When they left the jail around 10:30 p.m. and got into their station wagon, they left Philadelphia escorted by Deputy Price. Seasoned civil rights veterans such as James and Mickey were undoubtedly wary of being released from the jail at night, but they must have felt coerced by Price into doing so. They didn't stop to look for a public phone. Presumably, they just decided that getting to Meridian, approximately thirty-five miles away, as quickly as possible, was a priority. And Price undoubtedly wanted to make sure they didn't make a telephone call telling others where they were and what was happening.

The three turned off Highway 19 and drove on a side rode for several miles. After a while, Price stopped them, with a caravan of Klansmen driving behind him. Price said to the civil rights workers, "I thought you were going back to Meridian if we let you out of jail?" They replied that they were, and Price told them to get into his vehicle. As they did so, Price took his blackjack and struck James on the back of his head.

By this time, the three civil rights workers must have known they were in a grave situation. Rita would later say when asked about the risks Mickey assumed, "There was nothing masochistic about Mickey. He wanted to live: He loved life. He didn't want to die. He was as capable of fear as any young man. I have seen him afraid. It's true that he didn't fear a few days in jail. And he had no great fear of being slapped, kicked, or beaten. But to save his life, I think he would have done anything within his physical power. It's just that, even after all our talk of danger, Mickey Schwerner was incapable of believing that a police officer in the United States would arrest him on a highway for the purpose of murdering him, then and there, in the dark."

Horace Doyle Barnette

Barnette later recalled Cecil Price leading the Klan convoy:

> I followed Price down Highway 19, and he turned left onto a gravel road [Rock Cut Road]. About a mile up the road he stopped and [Jimmie] Snowden and I stopped behind him, with about a car length

between each car. Before I could get out of the car, Wayne [Alton Wayne Roberts] ran past my car to Price's car, opened the left rear door, pulled Schwerner out of the car, spun him around so that Schwerner was standing on the left side of the road, with his back to the ditch and said, "Are you that nigger lover?" and Schwerner said, "Sir, I know just how you feel." Wayne had a pistol in his right hand, then shot Schwerner. Wayne then went back to Price's car and got Goodman, took him to the left side of the road with Goodman facing the road, and shot Goodman. When Wayne shot Schwerner, Wayne had his hand on Schwerner's shoulder. When Wayne shot Goodman, Wayne was standing within reach of him. Schwerner fell to the left so that he was laying alongside the road. Goodman spun around and fell back toward the bank in back. At this time Jim Jordan said, "Save one for me." He then got out of Price's car and got Chaney out. I remember Chaney backing

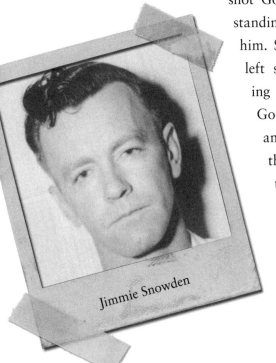

Jimmie Snowden

up, facing the road, and standing on the bank on the other side of the ditch and Jordan stood in the middle of the road and shot him. I do not remember how many times Jordan shot. Jordan then said, "You didn't leave me anything but a nigger, but at least I killed me a nigger." The three civil rights workers were then put into the back of their 1963 Ford wagon. I do not know who put the bodies in the car, but I only put Chaney's foot inside the car.

In another account, as the three men were awaiting their execution, several members of the lynch mob chanted

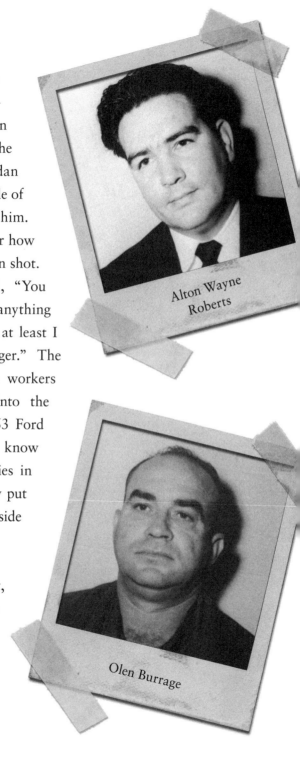

Alton Wayne Roberts

Olen Burrage

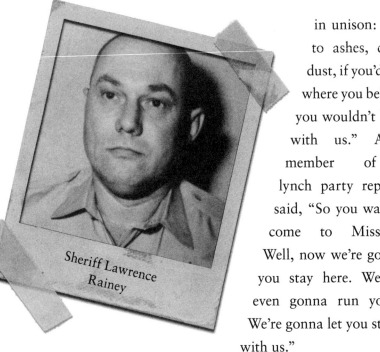
Sheriff Lawrence Rainey

in unison: "Ashes to ashes, dust to dust, if you'd stayed where you belonged, you wouldn't be here with us." Another member of the lynch party reportedly said, "So you wanted to come to Mississippi? Well, now we're gonna let you stay here. We're not even gonna run you out. We're gonna let you stay here with us."

According to Barnette, Olen Burrage then led the group to the earthen dam at the Old Jolly Farm, which he owned, to bury the bodies using a bulldozer. After the bodies were left at the earthen dam, Olen Burrage obtained a glass gallon jug and filled it with gasoline to burn the COFO vehicle.

At around 2:00 a.m. on Monday, June 22, Barnette and several Klansmen returned to Philadelphia, "and then someone said that we better not talk about this and Sheriff [Lawrence] Rainey said, 'I'll kill anyone who talks, even if it was my own brother.'" The men dispersed to their homes, perhaps thinking that the three young men would eventually disappear from the nation's consciousness. If they thought that, they were wrong.

CHAPTER 2
ANDREW GOODMAN

How dismally the day
Screams out and blasts the night.
What disaster you will say,
To start another fight.
See how heaven shows dismay
As her stars are scared away;
As the sun ascends with might
With his hot and awful light.
He shows us babies crying
We see the black boy dying
We close our eyes and choke our sighs
And look into the dreadful skies.
Then peacefully the night
Puts out the reddened day
And the jaws that used to bite
Are sterile where we lay.

 — Andrew Goodman, Spring 1964 Corollary to a Poem
 by A. E. Housman ("To an Athlete Dying Young")

On a summer day, a police car signaled the driver of a speeding car to pull over to the side of a country road. The stern police officer walked up to the car, leaned into the vehicle, and said to the driver: "Lady, do you know how fast you were going? And with all these little children in the car. You could go to jail for this. I could put you in jail for six months for driving at this rate of speed."

Suddenly, there was the sound of snuffling from the backseat of the car. A small boy was crying. "Andy, why are you crying?" his mother asked. "Mom, I don't want you to go to jail," came the reply. Carolyn Goodman's middle son, Andrew, or Andy as he was known to family and friends, was sensitive like his father.

Andrew Goodman was born in New York City on November 23, 1943. He had an older brother named Jonathan and a younger brother named David. His parents, Robert and Carolyn, met in the mid-1930s at Cornell University, where they were both undergraduate students.

Carolyn's father was a lawyer who was committed to social causes. He hired one of the first black lawyers to work in a New York City law firm. Carolyn obtained a degree from Cornell in home economics, and she would later obtain a master's degree in clinical psychology and a doctorate in education. Smart, beautiful, and strong, Carolyn began her political activism early. While she was at Cornell, she helped organize local farmers' cooperatives. In the late 1930s, she supported the Joint Anti-Fascist Refugee Committee, which

The Goodman brothers in 1956:
(*top to bottom*) David, Andrew, and Jonathan

assisted Spanish Republicans who had been exiled during the Spanish Civil War.

Robert, or Bobby as he was known, was intellectually curious and very much a Renaissance man who enjoyed writing poetry and wrote extensively about social issues. He loved learning and received not only a degree in literature from Cornell University but a civil engineering degree as well. Despite his love of literature, he went to work for his father's construction firm as a civil engineer. But his passion for literature, the arts, and social activism would always be a part of his life. A colleague would later say of Bobby Goodman that he was "that rare mixture of the practical businessman and the idealistic humanist."

A great influence on Andy and his extended family was Charles Goodman, Andy's grandfather. Charles's father came to the United States as an immigrant. His family was poor, and Charles was the only child in his family who went to college, where he studied to be a civil engineer. He founded the firm that would become the Grow Construction Company. Charles Goodman was responsible for many significant building projects in the New York City area. He cared less about money than working on the challenges of his engineering projects.

In 1933, Charles built a large house in upstate New York on 644 acres as well as several additional buildings at the south end of Tupper Lake in the Adirondacks. On this spacious compound, his two sons and three daughters, and their families, would escape the heat of the city and enjoy the summer. To Andy and his family, visiting Tupper Lake was a treasured family ritual. It was an idyllic rural retreat where Andy, his brothers, and the rest of the extended Goodman tribe swam, water-skied, hiked, canoed, read, sang, enjoyed communal meals, and generally hung out. Andy could usually be counted on to organize the other children to put on a play.

As Carolyn said of her father-in-law: "Grandpa Goodman had a profound impact on all of us." His values were inculcated into his family. Charles Goodman lived and loved the American dream: If you worked hard, were honest, and always did the best you could, the American system would reward you. Charles believed firmly in the Constitution of the United States and the ideas and ideals embodied in that document. That document applied to all Americans, not just some of them. "It's clear as a bell," he would say. Bobby and Carolyn strongly shared this value system and passed it on to their sons. David characterized his parents as constitutional fundamentalists who read the US Constitution

Charles Goodman in 1956 with Andrew, David, and Jonathan

literally, its rights guaranteed to all American citizens, not select groups.

Charles preached to his children and his ten grand-children the core Goodman family value: "Be a doer." It was essential to take action in support of your convictions and to give it your all. "He only showed respect to the doers," recalls David Goodman. "He was kind of polite to the people he didn't think were terribly productive. But you could tell he didn't think much of them." "Be a doer" was an admon-ishment that Andy, his brothers, and his cousins took to heart and applied to their own lives.

After they got married, Bobby and Carolyn Goodman moved into a large ten-room apartment on the Upper West Side of New York City. The sprawling apartment, filled with books and art, was a haven for artists, intellectuals, and pro-gressive politicians.

Andy grew up in a house-hold where free speech, independent thinking, equal rights for all, and noncon-formity were valued and encouraged. But the Goodmans' approach to discipline differed. Andy's father wasn't a disciplinarian and

Robert Goodman and his sons in 1956

never raised his voice to the boys. Carolyn didn't tolerate nonsense. As David Goodman would recall, "We got out of line, we knew it and we got back in line. Period. End of discussion. Over and out." Carolyn had a great influence on her sons. David added that "she instilled in all of us a great sense of self-reliance, self-respect, and — right, wrong, or indifferent — we thought we were invincible. That could be part of the reason why my brother went to Mississippi."

The Goodmans brought their distinctive personalities to their role as parents. Bobby had a keen interest in knowledge and learning. When he helped Andy and his brothers with their homework, he would become engrossed in the homework assignment as if he were the student. Carolyn valued discipline and made certain the boys completed their assignments. With their parents' influence, Andy and his brothers excelled at school.

But with their academic work came lessons in interacting with others. The Goodmans' neighborhood was a racially mixed community of black, white, and Hispanic families. Andy's mother recalled that "he played on the street and in the playgrounds with children who came from different cultures and races. He became aware at an early age of the differences in lifestyle and comfort between himself and his neighborhood friends. Even as a young boy, Andy had questions about these disparities. He saw the hopelessness and frustration of the newly arrived immigrants from Puerto Rico who had emigrated to the mainland to seek employment and a better life for their children. In discussions at home and in school he learned that language, color, and religion closed doors of opportunity to people already burdened by second-class education and poverty."

One of Andy's most notable attributes was his strong sense of fairness. For example, Andy had no tolerance for bullies. As his younger brother, David, noted, "It's strange, because in our family, nobody bullied him. It wasn't like he was on the receiving end of it." But when Andy observed someone being bullied, he would step into the situation and let people know that sort of behavior wasn't right, it wasn't fair. And you need to stand up to unfair people; it was just that simple. When David Goodman was a freshman at the Walden School, a private institution in Manhattan, two upperclassmen were picking on him. Andy heard about this and rounded the two up. Andy, a senior, told them he understood that they were pushing his younger brother around. They denied it. Andy replied, "Well, if you do, why don't you come and find me and try and push me around?" And that was the end of that. David saw Andy hit someone only once. "And the guy buckled. I think it was as much his passion as his strength." David recalled that "people respected my brother because he never abused his strength or good looks. He was very popular for that reason."

School also played an important role in Andy's life. The boys and all their cousins attended Walden School, which was considered an innovator in progressive education. The school placed a premium on tailoring education to the individual student, encouraging self-expression, and being concerned about the problems of society. During Andy's time at the school, the student body was predominantly Jewish (his family considered themselves Reform Jews), and many of their parents were refugees from Hitler's Germany.

Students developed strong views on social and political issues and were encouraged to express them. Unlike most schools at that time, Walden was antiauthoritarian in its approach to students, who were expected to address their teachers by their first names. By the standards of conventional education, the Walden School was a fairly permissive environment. But the students were taught that their opinions mattered. David Goodman characterized the school's approach to the individual student as "come up with your understanding of the way the world is, but make sure there's compassion in it and appreciation for what you have. And don't take it for granted."

Carolyn, Jonathan, and David were the "street smart" members of the family. Yet as the middle child, Andy played the role of mediator between his two brothers. Andy was more like his father, "sweet, thoughtful, sensitive . . . and handsome. He was much better-looking than either of us," recalled David. As Andy got older, his younger brother admired him for another reason: "He always brought the prettiest girls home."

Andy and his brothers took music classes at the Juilliard School, where Andy was instructed in playing the clarinet. He loved to play baseball, and he was an ardent Brooklyn Dodgers fan. David, who inherited his grandfather's interest in and aptitude for business, recalls that his brother also loved trading baseball cards, but "he was terrible at it." Jackie Robinson, who became the first black Major League Baseball player when he started playing with the Dodgers in 1947, was a friend of the Goodman family. Andy arranged for Robinson to come and speak to the student body at Walden, where the athlete was considered a hero.

The Goodmans had many friends in the theater and the performing arts. Theater became a passion for Andy, and an outlet for his creativity. He liked to write his own stories and plays. Richard Crosscup, the drama teacher at Walden, was impressed with Andy's dramatic skills during his years at the school. Crosscup also saw in Andy a person of sensitivity, insight, and compassion. He recalled an incident when Andy was in the sixth grade. A lonely boy got into a dispute at the school, and, overwhelmed, he ran home, saying he would never return. The other boys thought that only Andy could reassure the boy and bring him back to school, and he did.

Andy was particularly close to his cousin Jane Mark. Two years his junior, Jane thinks of the word *exuberance* when remembering her cousin. She remembers Andy as being fun to be with and upbeat. Within the broader dynamic of the Goodman family, Andy was considered stable, solid, respectful, as well as respected. "He really was protective and caring about other people," Jane recalled.

Jane and Andy attended Walden together, went to camp together, and sang together. Jane recalled fondly, "Andy was like my brother." Indeed, because Jane had no brothers, Andy was like a protective older brother. He offered his advice to Jane about the boys she was dating. And Andy once broke a date so he could attend one of Jane's basketball games. After family meals at Tupper Lake, they would sometimes escape and head down to the boathouse to talk. Jane recalls that when she was about fourteen years old she took up smoking cigarettes, to her older cousin's strong disapproval. Andy would launch into a lecture, but after a while, a grin would break out on his face and he'd say, "Why am I wasting my time on this?"

Goodman family members at St. Regis Lake in New York's Adirondacks in the mid-1950s: *(left to right)* Andrew, Carolyn, Robert, David, Annette Goodman Mark (Robert's sister), and Jane

Perhaps Andy's closest friend at Walden was Ralph Engelman. Ralph's parents were European Jews who came to the United States in 1939, and Ralph came to Walden at the beginning of his first year of high school. Andy had "an intellectually serious side" but was "also a very fun-loving person with a great sense of humor." After Andy's death, Ralph would recall that "[o]ne of the things I liked best about Andy was that when he was angry or ill at ease or happy, it was always beautifully obvious." Andy possessed a "unique combination of good-naturedness, of an ability to laugh with abandon" as well as an "intense seriousness and introspection." Ralph recalled Andy when he completed reading Tolstoy's voluminous work *War and Peace*, and how he talked about what Tolstoy had in mind writing the book and the ideas behind it. "Books mattered, ideas mattered to him."

Andy's family was a strong influence on him, but it wasn't going to dictate the course of his life. Ralph observed that his friend was in the process of blazing his own way in the world. Andy wasn't content to follow in anyone

At the Walden School, circa 1961 (*left to right*) Ruth Grunzweig, Andy, and Ralph

else's footsteps. As Ralph noted, "Andy was one of those rare individuals, rare in any generation, who were not satisfied with the wisdom and success they more or less inherited but did not have to struggle to achieve themselves. In other words, that background shaped him but didn't in any way define him, in that he went out and he was his own person."

Another important person in Andy's life was Ruth Grunzweig, who transferred to Walden in her sophomore year of high school. Ruth was the only child of parents who were refugees from the Holocaust and had come to America to rebuild their lives. Coming to Walden was an adjustment for Ruth. She had caught Andy's eye. During the summer before their junior year, Andy traveled around Europe with a youth group, and he wrote Ruth letters, telling her about what he was doing during his travels. During their junior year, they talked on the telephone and hung out together with a group of friends from school. Ruth thought of Andy as "a very regular guy and brighter than most, more talented than many, but he wanted to have fun." While he was fun-loving, there was a serious side as well. Andy was "the kind of person you could rely on," and he was "naturally oriented towards getting things done, towards working." She added, "I know for sure that Andy was about fifty times more mature than I was."

At Walden it was more common for people to go to movies and go out as part of a group of friends. That's the context in which Andy and Ruth spent much of their time together during their junior year. It was difficult to have a relationship in such a public space. But as time passed, Andy and Ruth carved out time away from their classmates. It was to become the first serious relationship for both of them. They took a number of excursions alone, visiting the Metropolitan Museum of Art or walking along the Hudson River in Riverside Park on Manhattan's Upper West Side. On an outing to the Bronx Zoo, Ruth recalled, "Andy first told me that he loved me." Their relationship intensified during their senior year, and they spent a great deal of time alone as a couple.

Andy's social activism came naturally through both his family and his school. Andy and several of his classmates were involved in the nuclear disarmament peace movement. Interest in the civil rights movement was a natural outgrowth of the common concern about social justice in Andy's world. In addition, there was also a strong sense of cultural connection and appreciation of the black contribution to American society, especially in the field of music. The jazz of the period was particularly important to Andy and his friends (e.g., the Modern Jazz Quartet, Thelonious Monk, and Miles Davis). They were huge fans of Ray Charles, whose hit song " 'What'd I Say' was almost like an anthem for the class," recalled Ralph Engelman.

During Andy's sophomore year at Walden, in the fall of 1958, Andy and Ralph decided to march in a rally for young people in support of school integration. The rally was sponsored by the Congress of Racial Equality (CORE), in Washington, DC, and half of the school decided to join them in participating in the march. Andy and Ralph demonstrated their independence by traveling alone together on a separate bus, away from adult supervision. Andy sat next to a black man on the bus, and they discussed the prospects for change in America's racial attitudes all the way to the nation's capital. The idealistic fifteen-year-old told Ralph as they got off the bus, "Boy is that guy a cynic."

The Walden School encouraged students to create their own study projects, and Andy and Ralph decided to visit West Virginia to learn firsthand about the rural poverty of Appalachia. In December of Andy's senior year, the two hopped on a Greyhound bus one evening after a school party, determined to make the most of their time in the Mountain State. The two seventeen-year-olds checked into a cheap hotel in the state capital of Charleston and immediately began interviewing officials. "That was an amazing experience. We spoke to everybody," Ralph Engelman recalled. The two cast a broad net and talked to state legislators, bankers, lawyers, and representatives of the United Mine Workers union. The two boys even called on the governor's mansion in the hope of seeing the governor, but they were unable to interview him.

They toured the state, and a retired union official showed them around a mining town where the mine had closed, destroying the town's economy. Andy and Ralph met with unemployed miners and their families. They saw a great deal of poverty, hunger, sickness, and despair. Andy and Ralph wanted to tour a coal mine, but they were prohibited from doing so because they were under eighteen years of age. As Ralph remembered the experience: "I think it just made more real in human terms what the issues were. I think there was a sense that these issues of poverty, of race, were very real, very tangible and involved real human beings. They were not abstract issues." When they returned to Walden, the two students presented their findings to a school assembly.

Later in their senior year, Andy and Ralph attended another assembly that featured several college students who had participated in the civil rights sit-ins in the South. The two had followed the use of sit-ins as a tactic in the civil rights struggle, and when it became used in New York in early 1960, the two young activists took the subway downtown after school and joined the picket line in front of the Woolworth's at Herald Square. Ralph recalled that their involvement reflected an "awareness that the problem of race was something very deep in our society and that it was in our backyard."

After senior year at the Walden School, Andy was accepted into the honors program at the University of Wisconsin–Madison. Ruth was going to attend Bennington College in Vermont. Andy headed off to Madison in the fall of 1961. He got a part in a theatrical production at the university but had to drop out of it when he came down with pneumonia and was confined to a bed in his dorm room. And before he could take the theater courses he wanted, Andy was told that he first had to make up the coursework he missed because of his illness. Andy was down about university life and anxious about his future. Early in 1962, Andy decided he'd had it. He returned home to New York City and decided to pursue his love for the theater. Andy took acting classes, and he was able to find work in several off-off-Broadway productions. He was an assistant stage manager, in the chorus of a musical, and had a small speaking role in a play called *The Chief Thing*. Andy thrived on his theater work and made several close friends. The exposure to people who devoted themselves to acting made him appreciate the challenges of such a career.

While Andy was exploring a theater career, he worked in his father's construction business. He helped work on the Alexander Hamilton Bridge between the Bronx and Manhattan during the summer of 1962. Andy demonstrated his strength one day when one of the construction workers, a black man who was larger than Andy, lost his footing and was clinging to the bridge by his fingertips. Andy pulled the man to safety, rescuing him from falling into the Harlem River.

Ultimately, Andy resumed his undergraduate work at Queens College, which was just a subway ride from both his home in Manhattan and New York's theater district. He felt comfortable at Queens, which had a strong drama department. Andy particularly enjoyed his courses in literature and anthropology. In the summer of 1963, Andy worked as a counselor at a camp in New Jersey where he taught drama to working-class young people. Someone there remembered Andy as a friendly, outgoing person who "resented unfriendly acts but not for any political reason, just as a kind of human,

THE 13TH ST. THEATRE

presents

Nicolas Evreinoff's

The CHIEF Thing

Directed by
Bro Herrod

a comedy for some,
a drama for others

Opening Performance
August 3, 1962

CAST

Paraclete	Sy Travers
Lady with the Dog	Marion Price
A Retired Clerk	John Seixas
A Dancer	Thelma Jones
An Actor	John M. Kelley
A Landlady	Eleanor Cody Gould
A Stenographer	Betty Aruda
A Student	Andy Goodman
A Theatre Manager	Greg Adams
A Stage Director	Edmond D. Collins
Electrician	J. P. Parker
Prompter	David Richman
The Voice	Harold J. Sypher
Nero	James Bartlett
Patronius	Jimmy Madden
Poppea	Karlene Wiese
Ligia	Irene Sypher
Lucian	Robert Patrick Sullivan
Comedian	Bernard Reed
Crispinilla	Peggy Morand
Nigidia	Joan Riggi
A Slave Girl	Lili Gonzales
A School Teacher	Antoinette Kray
The Silent One	Jann Kelley
A Fallen Woman	Irene Sypher

Masked Actors and Actresses and Guests:
Peggy Morand, David Richman, Karlene Wiese,
James Bartlett, Lili Gonzales, Jimmy Madden,
R. P. Sullivan, Joan Riggi

A program from *The Chief Thing*

Andy, with fellow cast members, is seated at the left.

compassionate thing. He didn't like bigotry for the same reason. His civil rights feelings had their basis in his humanity, rather than political feelings."

In the fall of 1963, Andy was entering his sophomore year of college, and he had largely decided against devoting his life to the theater. He changed his major to anthropology. Yet Andy still felt the tug of civil rights activism. He attended the March on Washington in August 1963, where Martin Luther King Jr. delivered his famous "I Have a Dream" speech. And his friend Ralph Engelman inspired Andy with the story of his participation in a Nashville sit-in and, later in 1963, with his description of the civil rights confrontations in Birmingham, Alabama. One can only imagine that hearing his friend's account of being on the front lines of the civil rights movement encouraged Andy's own commitment.

Andy's relationship with Ruth Grunzweig became more challenging as they attended universities in different states. During Ruth's first year at Bennington, they talked on the phone every Sunday and would get together when they were in New York City. After a time, Carolyn became concerned about the two seeing each other, apparently because she believed that Andy was too young to be in a serious relationship. Bobby and Carolyn passed this concern along to Andy. Andy "was not going to go against his parents' wishes," recalled Ruth. The situation made Ruth unhappy. But she realized that "Andy respected his parents. That sounds so uncool, right? But that didn't bother him. He had a handle on himself and on what he would and wouldn't do."

In early 1964, Aaron Henry, head of Mississippi's chapter of the NAACP, was on a recruiting tour of students for Freedom Summer, and he visited Queens College. He recalled Andy as being very much interested in the conditions in Mississippi and having "a very real desire to help." Before he left the campus from his visit, Henry remembered that "Andy told me he was definitely coming and thanked me for coming to Queens College and making him see his mission so clearly." Andy applied to be part of the Mississippi Summer Project and, after an interview with a northern SNCC worker, was ultimately accepted.

Volunteers for the Mississippi program were also required to have $150 with them and $500 available to pay for bail in case they found themselves in jail, which was a real possibility. Andy could have borrowed that amount from his parents, but he was determined to do it on his own. He got up early in the morning to load trucks for the United Parcel Service (UPS) to earn extra money in case he was selected to go to Mississippi. Andy's father recalled: "I, of course, would gladly have given Andy his money. But he made a point of working for it himself. He wanted his little contribution in Mississippi to be entirely his own."

Andy saw an opportunity to become involved in the 1964 World's Fair that was scheduled to open at Flushing Meadows on April 22, just a few miles from the Queens College campus. Some CORE activists were keen on using the event to protest civil rights concerns, but there was disagreement about how disruptive the protests should be. Andy and several hundred other Queens College students picketed New York City's pavilion on opening day.

As Andy's departure for Mississippi approached, the Goodmans held a going-away party for the family to wish him well. Andy pulled his cousin Jane aside and made her read a term paper he was finishing for a college sociology class on Malcolm X and the Black Muslim movement. Jane's opinion mattered to Andy. In the paper, Andy articulated his views on the race question and his understanding of the Black Muslims' animosity toward whites. He noted that "[t]he historical contempt that the white race held for the Negroes has created a group of rootless degraded people. The current neglect of the problem can only irritate this deplorable state of affairs." Jane thought the paper "astonishing. But at the same time I was thinking, Andy, there are all these people here to say good-bye to you, and he was so focused on this, which was wonderful to see."

Before he was accepted into the Mississippi program, Andy felt he had to tell his parents of his plans. Andy waited for one evening over dinner, when his two brothers were away from home, to broach the subject. He talked about the importance of the civil rights movement, the desirability of nonviolence as a tactic, and the need to be prepared to fight for what one believes to be right. Bobby and Carolyn had taught Andy and his brothers to stand up for social justice and act on their beliefs. Like most parents, they were worried that their child, even while doing something important and moral, would be injured or maybe even killed. But in many

Mississippi Summer Project

Name _Andrew Goodman_   Age _20_   Da

Address _██████████████████_   Pl

Occupation _Student - Queens College_

Business Address _____

List your home town and city newspapers

New York Times
(name)   (address)
New York Herald Tribune   _Daily_
National Guardian   ██████████████
The Nation   ██████████████

List the organizations to which you belong

(name)   (officer)   (address)

List your Senators

Jacob K. Javits   _Republican_
(name)   (party)

Kenneth B. Keating   _Republican_

Congressman:

William Fitts Ryan   _Democrat_
(name)   (party)

A page from Andy's Freedom Summer application

ways, Andy was proposing to do something they themselves had raised him to do. Why was he going? "Because," Andy stated, "this is the most important thing going on in the country. If someone says he cares about people, how can he not be concerned about this?" A fearful Carolyn forced herself to say, "It sounds like a great idea to me." She knew that she and her husband couldn't tell Andy not to act on his beliefs, after telling him the opposite all his life.

Carolyn later told journalist William Bradford Huie that Andy had decided to join the civil rights movement for two main reasons. Andy, she said, "felt it was unfair for him to enjoy so many good things without making some modest effort to help those who are unjustly deprived. And he felt that he had much to learn from the people in Mississippi. He never thought that he had all the answers."

Andy's older brother was concerned about Andy's safety in going to Mississippi and urged him not to go. Jane Mark's father — Andy's uncle — also warned him about how dangerous Mississippi would be for the sort of work Andy would be undertaking. He had spent part of his time in the army stationed in Mississippi during World War II, and he had observed firsthand how blacks were treated. Despite these warnings, Jane recalled that Andy didn't "look or seem afraid or particularly concerned. He just seemed resolute."

The night before Andy left for training in Oxford, Ohio, Ruth and Andy talked on the telephone. While they were no longer a couple, they had remained friends. They agreed to

April 14th/1964

To Whom It May Concern:

Andy Goodman has my permission to participate in the SNCC Program this summer, 1964, in Mississippi.

Mrs. Robert Goodman

Carolyn Goodman's permission note for Andy
to participate in Freedom Summer

take another try at their relationship when Andy returned from Mississippi in the fall.

The following morning, Bobby Goodman woke up his youngest son. His father never raised his voice, but David could tell his father was insistent that he get out of bed to say good-bye to Andy. Jonathan told him once again not to go. But Andy replied, "I'm going." Carolyn put some bandages and iodine in Andy's duffel bag, thinking that would repair the worst damage Mississippi could inflict on her son. Andy said good-bye to his family and walked out the door.

Andy's high school photo

Mr. and Mrs. Robert Goodman

████████

New York 24
New York

Dear Mom and Dad

I have arrived safely in Meridian
Mississippi. This is a wonderful town and
the weather is fine. I wish you were
here. The people in this city are wonderful
and our reception was very good.

All my love
Andy

When Andy arrived in Mississippi, he wrote his parents
to tell them that he arrived safely. The above postcard was
postmarked June 21, 1964, the last day of his life. It would
be the last communication his parents heard from him.

CHAPTER 3
JAMES CHANEY

There are those who are alive yet will never live. There are those who are dead yet will live forever. Great deeds inspire and encourage the living.

— Inscription on James Chaney's grave

In the early 1930s, an enterprising black man named James Chapel owned a thriving dairy farm in the general vicinity of Sand Flats, Mississippi. A white neighbor came to envy Chapel's success and wanted to buy the dairy farm. The neighbor repeatedly offered to buy the farm, but Chapel refused. Why should he sell it? He'd worked hard to make it prosperous, and he wanted to keep the farm in his family. But the white man became furious and threatened him. Chapel informed the man that he would shoot any white man who came onto his property uninvited. The angry man retreated, vowing vengeance.

Chapel knew he had taken a bold, if not dangerous, position with the neighbor, and he became obsessed with the fear that white vigilantes would burn his farm. He took to sitting on his front porch for hours at a time, cradling a shotgun and protecting his home and family. Finally, Chapel's concerned family urged him to leave the farm for a while and visit a married daughter in Alabama until the situation with the neighbor cooled off. Chapel got on the train to leave Mississippi, but he never reached his destination. The family later found out that a group of white men stopped the train and took Chapel off into the woods. He was never seen again. All that was found of him weeks after the abduction were his watch and his bloodied shirt next to the Chickasawhay River south of Quitman, Mississippi. By that time, Chapel's widow had sold the farm to the angry, envious white neighbor for far less than it was worth. If she hadn't, she knew that she, too, would have "come up missing."

James Chapel's abduction and murder was another reminder about the risks of being black in Mississippi. And it reinforced to his extended family — like so many black families — that security could never be taken for granted and they had to look out for one another. One member of James Chapel's family who would strongly adhere to that view was Fannie Lee Roberts. She didn't forget about Grandpa Jim and what the cost could be for blacks standing up for their rights. They, too, could "come up missing." She would place a premium on looking out for her family all of her life. She became Fannie Lee Chaney when she married Ben Chaney, who was working at a dairy farm outside of Meridian. After their first child, Barbara, was born, James Earl Chaney was born on May 30, 1943. Three more children would follow over the next decade: Janice, Julia, and Ben Jr.

After the couple married, Fannie Lee went to work as a

domestic servant in white homes — a profession that many black women in the South pursued. The workday of a domestic was long and hard, and the job paid little money. Typically, domestics were expected to arrive at the white home to cook and serve breakfast and then the rest of the day was spent cleaning, doing laundry, taking care of the family's children, and preparing and serving lunch and dinner. And then it was back home to take care of their own families. To make extra money, Fannie Lee sewed and took in laundry. Ben attended an agricultural and technical college, where he learned the trade of construction and plastering. He found work as a plasterer and traveled widely throughout Mississippi and the South.

Despite the seemingly endless struggle to pay the bills with a growing family, the Chaneys were determined that their children would receive a good education. They worked hard to pay the tuition for their children to attend Saint Joseph's Academy, a Catholic school that was the best education available to blacks in Meridian at that time. As Fannie Lee tired of the long hours as a domestic and the bus rides she needed to take to get to work, she took a job working as a lunchroom helper at a white school closer to home.

Hard work was another important family value. Her daughter Julia remembers that Fannie Lee was "an absolutely awesome individual in that here's a woman who ran several businesses with only the benefit of a fifth-grade education." Ben was frequently away from home as he was on the road working on plastering jobs. Accordingly, Fannie Lee came to depend on her two oldest children, Barbara and James. But when the two oldest were in charge, Julia recalled that James was "willing to allow Barbara Jean to be the heavy because he was ready to get out and play."

"J.E." was the family's affectionate name for James. His sister Julia remembers J.E. as "a fun-loving character. He was always a practical joker, although he was an excellent student." David Sims, who grew up next door to the Chaney family, recalls James as a prankster: "He liked to tell jokes, maybe put a match in your shoe and light it." Roscoe Jones remembers James as a bit of a ladies' man who was "very friendly, very laid back, very respectful."

Church was always important to the Chaney family, as well as the broader community in which they lived. James was a practicing Catholic, and he and his siblings went to mass on Sundays, and they would meet their mother at her Methodist church after mass. Julia recalled that "it would be well into the afternoon, around three p.m., before we were done with church" and that "every one of us was given kind of a cross-cultural religious experience."

Despite being somewhat small and severely asthmatic, James was athletic. He could run fast, and he loved to play contact sports — a continuing cause for concern to his mother. Once, when he was in high school, Fannie Lee was able to find the time to watch a football game in which James was playing. She couldn't stand to see her son getting knocked down on the playing field. In the middle of the game, she came onto the field to get her son out of the game. James was horrified. "Mama," he objected, "you can't come down here on the field like this!" Nothing would get in the way of protecting her children.

James felt as protective of his mother as she did of him. With his father's frequent absences, he was often the man of the house, and James took the role seriously. After everyone else had gone to bed for the evening, mother and son regularly stayed up late into the night talking. James was interested in electricity and science, and he had a strong aptitude for mechanics. He was skilled in making home repairs and enjoyed tinkering with the radio and other machines. Fannie Lee envisioned a career as an electrician for her son, if only he worked hard and applied himself.

The Chaney family lived in a black neighborhood in Meridian, which had a strong sense of community. But the harsh realities of life in a segregated society were inescapable. Julia doesn't recall her parents ever having an overt conversation with her and her siblings about surviving in a segregated society. "We never had [a conversation] because parenting in the South was about preparation, and our parents parented us in a way to prepare us to move outside of our insular communities and to go across town to school, because that's exactly where the Catholic school was." The Chaney children were taught to respect all adults, both black and white. They knew that white people were to be respected and "that we would not be mouthing off to them," but they wouldn't be mouthing off to any black adults, either. "So it wasn't that we were taught about what the risks were," she noted. "Our parents had the concern for those risks and what they did in raising us was damage control." The way they were raised brought them a measure of security. Julia stated that "I think we were so secure in knowing we were cared for, knowing there was family, knowing there was support, and prided ourselves in knowing how to behave in the general community." Nevertheless, the hostility of the white world was a constant presence.

When the Chaneys' eldest child, Barbara, was twelve years old, a white bill collector's son — who was approximately the same age — came to the Chaney family's home asking for payment. "Is Ben at home?" the boy asked. Barbara nodded, indicating her youngest brother who was nearby. The white boy made it clear that wasn't what he meant. "I mean your daddy." Barbara didn't appreciate that lack of respect for her father. "You call my daddy 'Mr. Chaney,'" she admonished the white boy. "Ben is a little boy." The next time the white bill collector talked to the elder Ben Chaney, he recommended that he beat his daughter for her disrespectfulness.

Ben Chaney, James's younger brother, recalled life in his Meridian neighborhood when he was growing up. "We lived across the street from a white family. From my side of the street on, it was the black community, and from their side of the street, it was the white community. Up until the time I was about ten years old, I always played with those white kids. But once I became ten, their parents came straight out and told me they didn't want me playing with their kids no more. Their mama told them they were better than I was and told me I couldn't associate with her son, and I had to call him 'Mister.' And the kids themselves adopted that attitude."

Because of financial concerns, by the time James had reached his early teens, he and his siblings had to attend public school. James went to Harris Junior College — a combination high school and junior college. In 1959, the sixteen-year-old James took a position on civil rights that got him into trouble. He attended an NAACP recruitment meeting in Meridian. The cost of membership was two dollars per person, a sum out of many people's price range. Being a

Ben and his mother, Fannie Lee Chaney, in August 1964

member of the NAACP was a sign of status in the black community, despite the fact that the Meridian chapter of the organization, like so many other branches throughout the South, did little more than collect membership fees.

James and several of his friends decided that the NAACP should do something more meaningful than collect membership fees. So they made and wore NAACP "buttons" made out of yellow paper. Dozens of others at the school followed suit. The school's principal was not sympathetic. The principal undoubtedly saw what James did not see, and that was the threat of retaliation from the school board. Fannie Lee supported her son's stand, but his father's reaction was decidedly different. James's father had spent a lifetime of hard work building goodwill with white employers in order to provide for the family. James's action threatened to undermine this goodwill and could potentially put his father's livelihood in jeopardy. The principal ordered the students to remove the buttons, but James and several of his friends refused. They were suspended from school.

James attempted to join the military, but he was rejected because of his asthma. He and a friend then decided to travel around and explore the South, and they went as far as Texas. James later went to work with his father on plastering jobs throughout Mississippi, Georgia, and elsewhere around the South. The work was hard, and the workdays were long. And James experienced firsthand the difficulties of living on the road as a black man. He and his father had to sit in the back of the bus wherever they went, purchase their food at grocery stores since most restaurants denied blacks service, and they had to stay at private black homes since most motels were restricted to whites.

But traveling with his father around Mississippi and the rest of the South was an important education for James. He was able to observe the political hierarchies of the many towns and counties he passed through, and James obtained a broader sense of the unfair, unequal way that black people were treated. When James came home to Meridian from his travels, he would ask, "Why do we live this way? Why do we have to live this way?" His sister Julia reflected, "That was his epiphany, I think, his burning question."

James would return to high school, but he did not stay long enough to graduate. His parents separated, and James went to work, often working with his father on plastering jobs. In 1962, Ben Chaney Sr. earned enough money to purchase an automobile, and James learned how to drive. James loved acquiring this new skill, which freed him from depending on public buses. He could go where he wanted, when he wanted. And with James's driving skills came a growing knowledge of the back roads of Mississippi.

In late 1963, James met with Sue Brown, who was several years younger and had attended his high school. Sue had been active in civil rights for several years and was currently working with young people in the Meridian chapter of the NAACP. She asked James if he was interested in meeting Matt Suarez, a young staff officer for CORE from New Orleans who had recently come to Meridian to begin a new civil rights effort in the area. Suarez needed help, and James volunteered. The two hit it off, and for the remainder of the year, James would serve as Suarez's primary assistant, driver, and guide to Meridian and the surrounding area. Suarez stressed to James that if they were ever to be chased on the road, he should be sure not to slow down or stop the car but hit the accelerator and outrun the pursuer — even if it was the police. Their lives could depend on it.

Most of the black people in the area were frightened to be seen with civil rights workers, and with good reason. So James became adept at navigating the back roads at night and learned to make an effective appeal to a reluctant recruit in a short amount of time. James regularly canvassed black ministers throughout Mississippi, trying to persuade the preachers to permit their churches to be used as freedom schools to prepare the local blacks to make their applications to vote. He would pose his question, "Why do you think we have to live this way?" And then he would discuss some of the things that could be done to enable black people to vote. As a black man and a native of Mississippi, James had particular credibility because he was no stranger to this environment.

When Rita and Mickey Schwerner came to Meridian in January 1964, James was one of the first to help them get settled as they set about establishing the community center in the city. He then went off to help Matt Suarez prepare for Canton's Freedom Day, to encourage the local black community. After spending about six weeks there and elsewhere around the state, James returned to Meridian as a seasoned, full-time civil rights worker, and he began his close work with the Schwerners. All of James's civil rights work, both prior to working with Mickey and Rita and everything he did after meeting them, was about preparation for Freedom Summer.

As James came to know the Schwerners, so did the Chaney family. James's sister Julia recalled that the Schwerners were "in and out of our house as often as J.E. was, so they were kind of an ancillary part of the family," and they shared in many family meals. Mrs. Chaney assisted in the community center's clothing drive and other activities, and other family members visited the center as well. Julia fondly remembers the Schwerners as "a wonderful couple. And I kind of viewed them in awe because here was this young white couple coming into Mississippi to challenge the law for people of color, for people like myself. So the community certainly embraced them and revered them." She recalls the Schwerners "having such wonderful energy and were so easy to connect with, because they weren't people who were evidencing any status. They weren't people who were coming to rule anyone or anything. They just came from this human space, this very human space."

James quickly became indispensable to the Schwerners and their civil rights work, and they believed his hard work and dedication deserved to be acknowledged. The Schwerners and another colleague appealed to CORE headquarters to make James formally a part of the CORE staff. In April

1964, they wrote national headquarters that "[t]here is no distinction in our minds or his as to the amount of work he should do as a volunteer, and we as paid staff. We consider James part of the Meridian staff, and he is in on all major decisions which are made here. . . . James has never so much as asked us to buy him a cup of coffee, though he has no means of support. We believe that since he long ago accepted the responsibilities of a CORE staff person, he should be given now the rights and privileges which go along with the job."

James embraced the civil rights movement's use of nonviolence. It came naturally to him, since his first reaction was not to be violent. As an adolescent, James was not an antagonist in conflicts. Instead, he "could talk people down," encouraging people to hear each other out and back off from physical conflict. Nevertheless, he knew that his civil rights work was dangerous.

James's father was concerned about the risks of his son's civil rights activities and warned him. "Boy, you know you can get yourself killed." But James was just as adamant that he understood what he was doing. For the elder Ben Chaney, the question "Why do we have to live this way?" was a question he never attempted to answer. He had carved out a niche for himself in Mississippi society that allowed him to do what was necessary to provide for his family.

When James came back to Meridian to be with his mother and siblings after each of his civil rights trips, he would tell them about his experiences. If it was night when he returned,

Fannie Lee Chaney in her home with a photo of James behind her

Julia recalled that "we would turn the lights off and sit on the living room floor, because it was away from the windows." The Chaneys knew the dangers that James faced in taking on civil rights work. But before James left the house to continue with his work, he and his mother would have the same conversation. His mother would ask, "Boy, you know what you're doing?" And James would always reply, "Yes." "You know what can happen to you," his mother would warn.

The entire Chaney family realized that James was taking an enormous risk. His sister Julia recalled, "And for him it was not escaping the risk, because he knew eventually, at some point, there was going to be a major clash. And he had resolved himself to understanding it may be something that he did not survive. But it did not sway him. It did not stop him. And it did not change him."

Working closely with Mickey, James was kept busy throughout the first half of 1964, reaching out to the black community, organizing boycotts and demonstrations, and, inevitably, being arrested by the local authorities. Young Ben Chaney would become active in the civil rights movement as well. It was another close bond between the brothers. James would take Ben to get his hair cut and got him his first football uniform. Ben adored his older brother. His sister Julia observed that patterning his behavior after his older brother was not surprising, since Ben was James's shadow. "My mother was okay with that to some degree, and when she felt that it was not okay she would let him know and that would be the end of that, even though it would aggravate Ben."

Ben recalled that "[w]hatever my brother wanted to do or did, I wanted to do. Mickey and Rita organized the community center in the spring, and I went every day. I was in school at the time, and usually after school I would come by the center. Sometimes my brother would bring me home. I was eleven years old. I played with the typewriter, played Ping-Pong, sang freedom songs. 'Keep Your Eyes on the Prize' was my favorite. The one I disliked the most was 'We Shall Overcome.' It was so slow."

For Ben, involvement in the civil rights struggle was not only involvement in an important cause but also a chance to be with his brother:

It was okay to be hit. It was okay to go to jail. I was arrested more than twenty-one times before I was twelve years old. "Demonstrating without a permit." That was what they locked everybody up for. Because I was a juvenile, only eleven for most of my arrests, I would go to jail, and then they would put me in a holding cell, or they would set me on a bench right outside the courtroom. We would wait until an adult came and got us out. In a couple of demonstrations, Mickey Schwerner would come and get me out. Most of the time it would be my brother. He was pretty quiet, but I remember waiting one time for him to come and get me. I could hear his steps in the hallway, and he was saying, "I come for my brother." I was glad. He was proud of me. I was glad to be there too.

Like all civil rights workers in Mississippi, the arrival of Freedom Summer would pose a great challenge and risk to James Chaney. But he was willing to meet that challenge and accept that risk. "Why do we have to live this way?" was the question he asked himself and others in Mississippi's black community. He was committed to helping destroy segregation, and Freedom Summer was going to be an important step in that process.

CHAPTER 4

MICHAEL SCHWERNER

One day . . . you might find something worth dying for. Freedom is worth dying for, fighting for other people's freedom.

— Mickey Schwerner

In 1957, when Mickey Schwerner was eighteen and getting ready to leave his home in Pelham, New York, to go off to college, he told his mother that he was planning on buying a Volkswagen. His mother said, "Mickey, are you sure you want to buy a German-made car? You know about Auschwitz and you know that some of your relatives were murdered there. So soon after Auschwitz, are you sure you'll feel comfortable driving a Volkswagen?"

"I know how you feel, Mother," Mickey replied. "One reason I want to buy it is that it is a very economical and practical car. But, more important, I want to spend my life relieving hate, not preserving it. I see reason to hope that there will never be another Auschwitz." Mickey saw post–World War II Germany moving past the Hitler-era Holocaust that had claimed the lives of millions, including some of his family members, and moving toward a far more positive future. He wanted to demonstrate his belief that the future of humankind was moving upward and forward.

Michael Henry Schwerner was born in New York City on November 6, 1939. He and his older brother, Stephen, were the children of Nathan Schwerner, a partner in a wig manufacturing company that had been in the family for many years, and Anne, who had taught biology in high school. Both Nathan and Anne were liberal activists who also worked as union organizers. Nathan had been a member of the War Resisters League — the oldest secular pacifist organization in the United States. In 1947, the family moved to Pelham, New York, which was known for the high quality of its public schools.

Steve and Mickey were taught to respect all races and value all people. "We grew up in a family that believed in social justice. That's what we were taught as little kids," Steve Schwerner recalled. The boys were taken to New York Yankees baseball games, but they went to watch the Negro baseball leagues as well.

Michael "Mickey" Schwerner

Both Mickey and his brother loved sports, and in high school, Mickey played sports throughout the school year. He also enjoyed rock music. Mickey loved animals from the time he was a boy, and other children in the neighborhood would come to him for assistance with sick or lost pets.

Investigative journalist William Bradford Huie wrote of Mickey's humanism:

> Perhaps he believed so tenaciously in Man because he did not believe in God. He insisted that he was an atheist; that he believed in All Men rather than in One God. His grandparents had been European Jews; but his parents, both born in the United States, had begun moving within Judaism to humanism, and Mickey continued the movement when at thirteen he decided not to observe the bar mitzvah ritual. He was not a Jew, he was only a man. He didn't believe in original sin but in original innocence. Because he held no hope of heaven, he held extravagant hopes for the earth. Because he had no God to love, he loved God's creatures all the more.

Mickey spent his freshman year of college at Michigan State University in East Lansing, Michigan. For his sophomore year, he transferred to Cornell University in Ithaca, New York, where he attended the College of Veterinary Medicine to pursue his longtime interest in caring for animals. He studied veterinary medicine for several semesters, then changed course to major in rural sociology. While at Cornell, Mickey led a successful effort to pledge a black student to his fraternity.

When Mickey was home at Pelham in the summer before his final year at Cornell, a friend introduced him to a petite eighteen-year-old woman named Rita Levant, who was about to begin her sophomore year at the University of Michigan, where she was majoring in education. Having a long-distance relationship was challenging, but the two formed a strong enough bond to stay in close touch during the following school year. After Mickey's graduation from Cornell in June 1961, he made plans to begin a graduate degree in social work at the Columbia University School of Social Work in New York City. Rita transferred to nearby Queens College, where she was closer to Mickey. By the end of his first year at Columbia, Mickey had become disenchanted with what he thought of as the school's limited approach to social work. He felt that one of the root causes of poverty was racism, and the school didn't address such important issues. Mickey was impatient for action in the area of civil rights, and he wanted to fight bigotry and bring about a more just society.

So in June 1962, Mickey left school and became a social worker in a public housing project in the Lower East Side of Manhattan. Mickey made an even more important commitment to the future at that time when he and Rita got married at the Schwerner home in Pelham. The newlyweds moved into an apartment in Brooklyn and began a new life together.

A caring person, Mickey was innately respectful and tolerant of others. He had a natural aptitude for social work. Mickey ran an after-school program, where he demonstrated a special rapport with troubled adolescents. He took to wearing a goatee to make himself look older.

Mickey came to view social work — important and challenging as it was — as inadequate to address social change. He became convinced that political activism was an essential adjunct to the work he was undertaking as a social worker. In early 1963, he became involved in a chapter of CORE in New York's Lower East Side. He also joined and became involved in other organizations working for civil and human rights.

During this time, Rita kept busy with her college studies as well as volunteer work. She joined the same CORE chapter as Mickey. And as the year progressed, the Schwerners became more committed to the civil rights movement. On July 4, 1963, Mickey joined a CORE-sponsored sit-in at a segregated amusement park outside of Baltimore, Maryland. He was arrested and spent two days in jail. A week later, both Mickey and Rita were arrested for disorderly conduct when they and several others stepped in front of a cement truck at a construction site as part of a protest against racial discrimination in New York City's building trade unions.

With the growing intensity of the civil rights struggle in the South, Mickey became determined to join the front lines in the fight for civil rights. Mickey applied to CORE's national office to work in the South. Rita was to receive her college diploma in January 1964, freeing both of them to start a new life elsewhere in the civil rights movement. In his application to CORE, Mickey articulated his commitment:

I am now so thoroughly identified with the civil rights struggle, that I have an emotional need to offer my services in the South. As a social worker I have dedicated my life to social ills; however, my profession, except in isolated instances, as yet has not become directly involved in the most devastating social disease at the present time — discrimination. I also feel that the Negro in the South has an even more bitter fight ahead of him than in the North and I wish to be a part of that fight. In essence, I would feel guilty and almost hypocritical if I do not give full time for an extended period. . . . The vocation for the rest of my life is and will be to work for an integrated society. I plan to do this work primarily in New York City where my roots are, but I feel it is important that I have a first-hand understanding of how people in other sections of the country specifically are affected by prejudice and how discrimination is being dealt with. I want to know and work with the "people" not just read about situations or take some[one] else's subjective view. I want to be there first-hand. Therefore, I see working for CORE in the South as an educational experience that can be obtained in very few other ways.

In her application to CORE, Rita indicated her wish to work with Mickey. She stated that it was her hope to "someday pass on to the children we may have a world containing more respect for the dignity and worth of all men than that world which was willed to us."

The Schwerners received word that they'd been accepted as CORE field workers in the South on Thanksgiving Day 1963, just days after the national trauma of President Kennedy's assassination. After settling their affairs and packing, Mickey, Rita, and another white CORE member hired to work in Mississippi left New York City behind and drove to the Magnolia State, arriving on January 16, 1964. They were the first full-time white civil rights workers in the state.

Roscoe Jones recalls meeting the Schwerners for the first time. Mickey was "a little short guy, with a beard." He "wasn't talking much but had a personality out of this world," and Rita "was skinny as a pencil." Roscoe remembered that "the black leadership accepted them very well. Yeah, Mickey had a way." Roscoe was one of the young black leaders in the local community Mickey was to train. "Mickey was committed. Mickey trained me personally in nonviolence. And he would take me around with him and he would introduce me to people, and he always reminded me, 'Roscoe, you're a leader, be very careful of what you do and how you do it.' "

The affable Mickey fit in well with the veteran civil rights workers, and readily accepted the movement's emphasis on making decisions by consensus and the need to develop local leadership. Along with Rita's firm commitment to the movement and her strong organizational skills, the Schwerners made a strong, mutually supportive team. The couple was tasked with taking over responsibility for the new community center in Meridian, along with other programs.

To adjust to the new environment, Mickey shaved off his beard, knowing that it would make him even more conspicuous among the white residents who valued conservative appearance. Still, "outside agitators" like Mickey eventually became the focus of attention in a generally hostile white community.

Housing became a headache for the couple. When they first arrived in Meridian, Mickey and Rita stayed with three or four black families, but the Schwerners had to move because the families "received intimidating phone calls and became afraid to house us," recalled Rita. They were then able to rent a house but were evicted in early June and had to find an apartment.

By the end of February 1964, Meridian's community center was up and running and the first few young black people began to come by. The young New Yorkers had worked hard to establish the center, relying on local volunteers. Rita cheered up the spaces with paint and curtains, and she used her considerable organizational skills to solicit contributions of office supplies and books — many from New York publishing houses. She would later give sewing classes. The center's library would ultimately boast approximately ten thousand volumes. Mickey, James Chaney, and other volunteer carpenters were challenged to build enough bookshelves to keep pace with the flood of book donations to the center.

Local children in front of the community center in
Meridian during Freedom Summer

For those who came by, the center offered story hours for
children; a game room for teenagers, with a Ping-Pong table
and a phonograph; refreshments, transportation, voter registration classes for adults; and training to apply for clerical
and civil service jobs. Posters and leaflets were distributed at
neighborhood stores, restaurants, and churches to make the
center's activities known in the local black community.
CORE provided the community center with a blue Ford station wagon that James used frequently, and he became adept
at navigating the country roads in the surrounding counties.
Inevitably, the local white community became increasingly
aware of the center's activities.

Larry Martin was a frequent visitor to the new community center, which was across the street from where he lived. He was eleven years old when the Schwerners came to Meridian. "I spent lots of time with Mickey and Rita. They were funny, most always happy. He used to do a lot of magic tricks for us. He'd take Ping-Pong balls in his hands and say, 'It's over here,' and pull it from somewhere else. It fascinated us. We had never seen that before." He saw a lot of James Chaney as well. "James was a nice, easygoing fella, quiet most of the time. Come around with his hands in his overalls. He wore a blue T-shirt. He was real friendly. He was different from most black guys you'd see. Most guys would be hanging in the pool rooms or hanging on the corner. But he was up there. He had his job to do. Always seemed to be happy and ready to work."

Although he was a white New Yorker, Mickey could relate to the challenges Mississippi blacks faced. Julia Chaney noted, "Now don't think that Mickey came to the South green. He wasn't. He was a social worker. He had experienced the pain of broken lives just from that perspective. He had to know a few things about African Americans' lives even if it was in New York." He knew about the pain and suffering of others as a social worker. "Which is where the caring came from," she added. Rita shared this commitment to help others. "He was this young man who had the capacity to care beyond his own concerns, beyond his own risk, and a young lady who supported him and also evidenced the same capacity of caring. That was most profound. That is the connection, why it was so easy for Mickey and J.E. to make a connection, to have a bond almost immediately." Indeed, James and Mickey formed an unusually close bond. Julia Chaney stated that "it was great to see them chatting and laughing as well as questioning and challenging each other, and to know that Mickey respected him." If it was an unknown or critical situation, Mickey would defer to James and accept his recommended course of action.

Mickey, along with James Chaney and other volunteers, ventured out into Meridian's surrounding communities to recruit people to attend voter registration classes. An early test case regarding equal access to public places was an attempt to integrate a white church in Meridian. The couple recruited Sue Brown from the community center to attend a service. The Schwerners dropped her off, wearing her Sunday finest, several blocks from the church. The church leaders had clearly been tipped off, and a small group of deacons awaited the young woman. When she expressed her desire to worship at their church, one of the deacons replied that she could only worship in the church basement. She declined. One of the deacons explained to her, "Blackbirds and red-birds are all God's creatures, but they travel in separate flocks. Young lady, God didn't mean for black and white to be together."

There were many white citizens in the Meridian area who had a far more combative view about racial integration than the church deacons. And in a fairly short amount of time, the Schwerners were the target of their hostility. Mickey was occasionally picked up by the cops and taken to the police station to be questioned about the couple's activities. Obscene and threatening telephone calls were made to them. Rita recalled that "[b]y May we received so many phone calls at late hours of the night that in order to get some sleep we were forced to remove our telephone receiver before going to bed." The threatening phone calls were particularly frightening, "such as someone calling and telling me that he was planning to kill my husband, or that my husband was already dead. Michael received anonymous calls telling him that they intended to kill me or that I was already dead." A store owner close to the center of town was constantly abusive to the Schwerners, referring to Mickey as "Jew-boy" and "nigger lover," and their car was frequently followed by police cars and other local whites. The Schwerners did not allow these mounting threats to deter them from their work, as heavily as it must have weighed on them. Mickey maintained his upbeat and friendly demeanor. But the threat of violence was always present.

With every new initiative they sponsored, the Schwerners became more prominent and therefore more of a target for the segregationists. On the first Sunday in March 1964, the Schwerners integrated a white church. At the invitation of the church's minister, the Schwerners and two black women attended the church service. While there were no incidents at the service, it was considered an unwanted invasion by many in the white community. The local newspaper, the *Meridian Star*, negatively editorialized the integrated church service,

"If we want to preserve segregation, why don't we wake up and do something about it."

By at least March 1964, the Meridian Police Department and the Sovereignty Commission were monitoring Mickey and his activities. In a Sovereignty Commission report, a commission investigator stated that "both Michael and Rita Schwerner are in Meridian working for CORE. Their purpose there is evidently to contact local Negroes for the purpose of encouraging them to register to vote and also to teach them how to pass the voter registration examination. . . . Chief O. A. Booker, Detective G. L. Butler, and the sheriff's office of Lauderdale County are cooperating in this matter by keeping these subjects under surveillance and are getting information from reliable informants." Clearly, local officials were not going to be helpful to the Schwerners. And since many of the local officers were either members of, or sympathetic to, the Ku Klux Klan, information about the Schwerners' activities and whereabouts was invaluable to those determined to do harm to them.

With James Chaney's assistance, Mickey was able to accelerate voter registration efforts in Meridian and surrounding locales such as Clarke County and the notoriously tough Neshoba County, where Mickey noted that "no Negro has been registered since 1955." However, Mickey had befriended an enthusiastic supporter in his civil rights efforts in Cornelius Steele, who lived in the rural Longdale area of Neshoba County. Steele was eager to help out with the voter registration effort and believed there was enthusiasm in the local black community to set up a freedom school and community center for the rapidly approaching summer project. Largely because of Steele's encouragement, Mickey made approximately thirty trips to Neshoba County between February and June 1964, with James often accompanying him. Because of the risk involved in traveling to and from this hostile outpost, the two adhered to a rigid security protocol and would telephone Meridian if they were running late. Rita always insisted on staffing the telephones when the two were out on the road.

Once, Rita asked to accompany the two men on one of their trips to Philadelphia, the county seat of Neshoba County, but James was adamantly opposed to the idea. He explained to his white friends the facts of life in Neshoba County, a notoriously hostile place for the civil rights movement, where the local law enforcement officers were on the lookout for civil rights activists and outside agitators. Rita recalled James telling her "that if I went, he would not, as he said that if he was seen in Neshoba County with a white woman, we would all be killed." It was that simple. Rita stayed in Meridian.

Undeterred, Mickey moved forward with an ambitious plan to demonstrate against three stores in Meridian that relied heavily on black business but refused to hire blacks or to permit them to be served at the stores' lunch counters. After training volunteers in nonviolent protest, Mickey drove several dozen protesters to one of the stores on April 25, where they were largely successful in keeping black consumers away. When the demonstration was resumed several days later, the police arrested the demonstrators. Mickey was observing the demonstration from his car, where he was sitting with James. Mickey, who had regrown his beard, was charged with "obstructing a crosswalk with an automobile" and taken into custody.

Mickey wanted to be jailed with his black colleagues, but he was placed in a cell with white prisoners. A police officer took one of Mickey's white cell mates aside to have a word with him. When the white prisoner returned to the cell, he pulled Mickey aside and said, "I don't know who you are or what you do. But while you're in this jail, you'd better keep quiet about it." Mickey asked, "What did the cop say?" The white prisoner reiterated that no one would stop them if he and the others wanted to give Mickey a beating.

Mickey served his three days of jail time without being harmed, but when the demonstrations resumed in late May, he was arrested again. While he was being booked at the police station, a Klansman came up to him and said, "You must be that Communist-Jew nigger lover they call Goatee." Despite such hateful comments, Mickey continued with his work.

The looming Freedom Summer influx of outside activists and Mickey's growing success served as a huge recruiting tool for the White Knights of the Ku Klux Klan. Unbeknownst to Mickey, in March 1964, plans to kill him had been hatched at state and local Klan meetings. In late March, the Lauderdale

Klan had voted to concur with the vote of state KKK officials to eliminate Mickey. Klan members subsequently watched Mickey closely after that, looking for an opportunity to murder him. With every initiative Mickey launched, the Klan's determination to stop him increased.

CHAPTER 5
THE LONG SUMMER

You don't know the Deep South like I do. Mississippi isn't like Georgia or the Carolinas. You've never seen hate like a Mississippi white boy can hate. They'd kill you in a minute.

— Author Pat Conroy recounting what his Georgia-born mother said in refusing to give permission for him to participate in the 1964 Freedom Summer project

Fannie Lee Chaney was worried. It was late Sunday afternoon and James and his friends hadn't come home from Neshoba County or even called. When she called the community center in Meridian, she was alarmed to learn that no one had heard from the three young men. Fannie Lee feared the worst: that James, like his great-grandfather, had gone missing.

David Goodman woke up early on Monday, June 22, in his family's Manhattan apartment for the first day of his summer job. He was going to head to the subway to go to work at one of his father's construction sites. The living room in the apartment was huge with large windows. It was almost never used, except when Carolyn Goodman was entertaining guests. But that's where David found her alone that morning.

She was "lost-looking," David recalled. "And I could tell there was something the matter — something devastatingly the matter." He said nothing to his mother, he just looked at her. "And she said, 'Your brother's missing.' That was it. . . . I was devastated. I knew it was serious."

Rita Schwerner was awakened in her dorm room in Oxford, Ohio, around one that Monday morning. She was told to come to the school office, where she took a telephone call from Jackson, Mississippi, and was informed that the three men were missing and presumed to be in a Mississippi jail. Later that morning, Rita was told that the three had been detained at the Neshoba County jail and subsequently released. They were now considered "missing."

COFO workers had been spreading the word that the three civil rights workers were missing since their failure to return to Meridian. They stressed the gravity of the situation, the hostility and lack of assistance typical from local authorities, and the corresponding urgent need for federal assistance in helping to locate the three men. The national news media was intensely interested in this story and swarmed over Mississippi to cover it. Andy's and Mickey's parents discussed plans to fly to Washington, DC, the next day to lobby for the federal government to do everything possible to find the three young men.

At Oxford, Bob Moses addressed the next group of several hundred volunteers who were about to begin their week of training for the Freedom Summer project in Mississippi. As he was discussing the importance of nonviolence, one of

MISSING

THE FBI IS SEEKING INFORMATION CONCERNING THE DISAPPEARANCE AT PHILADELPHIA, MISSISSIPPI, OF THESE THREE INDIVIDUALS ON JUNE 21, 1964. EXTENSIVE INVESTIGATION IS BEING CONDUCTED TO LOCATE GOODMAN, CHANEY, AND SCHWERNER, WHO ARE DESCRIBED AS FOLLOWS:

| **ANDREW GOODMAN** | **JAMES EARL CHANEY** | **MICHAEL HENRY SCHWERNER** |

	ANDREW GOODMAN	JAMES EARL CHANEY	MICHAEL HENRY SCHWERNER
RACE:	White	Negro	White
SEX:	Male	Male	Male
DOB:	November 23, 1943	May 30, 1943	November 6, 1939
POB:	New York City	Meridian, Mississippi	New York City
AGE:	20 years	21 years	24 years
HEIGHT:	5'10"	5'7"	5'9" to 5'10"
WEIGHT:	150 pounds	135 to 140 pounds	170 to 180 pounds
HAIR:	Dark brown; wavy	Black	Brown
EYES:	Brown	Brown	Light blue
TEETH:		Good; none missing	
SCARS AND MARKS:		1 inch cut scar 2 inches above left ear.	Pock mark center of forehead, slight scar on bridge of nose, appendectomy scar, broken leg scar.

SHOULD YOU HAVE OR IN THE FUTURE RECEIVE ANY INFORMATION CONCERNING THE WHEREABOUTS OF THESE INDIVIDUALS, YOU ARE REQUESTED TO NOTIFY ME OR THE NEAREST OFFICE OF THE FBI. TELEPHONE NUMBER IS LISTED BELOW.

Edgar Hoover

DIRECTOR
FEDERAL BUREAU OF INVESTIGATION
UNITED STATES DEPARTMENT OF JUSTICE
WASHINGTON, D. C. 20535
TELEPHONE, NATIONAL 8-7117

June 29, 1964

The disappearance of Andy, James, and Mickey set off an enormous manhunt that captivated the nation during the summer of 1964. This FBI "Missing" poster became the iconic symbol of this major civil rights case.

the staff came to the side of the stage and quietly informed Moses about the three missing men. He walked back to the center of the stage and stared at the floor for several minutes as the volunteers in turn stared at him with growing concern. After he composed himself, Moses spoke quietly to the group: "Yesterday morning, three of our people left Meridian, Mississippi, to investigate a church burning in Neshoba County. They haven't come back, and we haven't had any word from them. We spoke to John Doar in the Justice Department. He promised to order the FBI to act, but the local FBI still says they have been given no authority."

As he lapsed into silence in front of the increasingly concerned audience, Rita Schwerner came to the podium to pass along what was known so far about the incident and to urge the volunteers to contact their members of Congress and demand federal assistance in finding the men, and to get their parents to do the same. "And then she left, and she was very emotional," Bob Moses recalled. "I spoke after her. I waited until she left, because we had to tell the students what we thought was going on. If, in fact, anyone is arrested and then taken out of the jail, then the chances that

Bob Moses *(far left)* and Willie Peacock *(far right)* in Mississippi in 1962

they are alive were just almost zero. We had to confront the students with that before they went down [to Mississippi], the fact that as far as we could see, all three of them were dead. And that they had to make the decision now as to whether they really wanted to carry through on this and go down. We sang a couple of songs, and for a while I was worried because no one was leaving. But finally a few of them did leave, so I did think that the message had gotten through."

The disappearance of the three men cast a shadow over Freedom Summer, but the volunteers traveled to Mississippi and participated in the program. And many of Mississippi's black citizens embraced the volunteers that summer, risking a great deal by bringing them into their homes and working with them on the voter recruitment and education initiatives.

With news of the disappearance, James Farmer, head of CORE; George Raymond, CORE's Mississippi field secretary; entertainer and civil rights activist Dick Gregory; and John Lewis of SNCC, met up in Meridian with the goal of traveling to Neshoba County to find out what happened to the three civil rights workers. Meridian police attempted to dissuade Farmer and his colleagues from going to Philadelphia. One of the senior police officials warned him, "Farmer, don't go over there. That's one of the worst redneck areas in this state. They would just as soon kill you as look at you. We cannot protect you over there." But their group, totaling thirty-five, was determined to go to Neshoba County. They formed a car caravan and headed to Philadelphia. When they reached the city limits, a squadron of police cruisers met them. Sheriff Rainey stepped out from one of the vehicles, with a wad of tobacco in his cheek. He informed them they would be escorted into town by his deputy sheriffs, some of whom were carrying shotguns.

When the caravan rolled up to the courthouse in Philadelphia, Lewis recalled that the town square "looked like an armed camp. Dozens of men in short sleeves roamed around with guns and rifles in their hands — local men who had been deputized by Rainey." All around the square were policemen with rifles, including on rooftops. When Sheriff

On June 21, 1965 — the one-year anniversary of the murder of the three civil rights workers — Fannie Lee Chaney and James Farmer sit amid the charred ruins of the Mount Zion Methodist Church during memorial services.

Rainey stepped out of his car, he informed the visitors that he would meet with only four of them. Raymond, Lewis, Farmer, and Gregory followed him and Deputy Sheriff Price into the old courthouse. They rode silently in the elevator with Rainey and Price and entered into a hot, stuffy office with a ceiling fan slowly working. Three men were waiting for them, a representative of the state police and two local attorneys. Lewis recalled the tense atmosphere. "Rainey and Price did nothing to hide their contempt for us. They sneered. They smirked."

If James Chaney, a black man, was the only person who turned up missing in Neshoba County in June 1964 under suspicious circumstances, it probably would have received little, if any, media attention outside of Mississippi. But because two of the men were white and from New York City, it became not only a major New York story but a national story as well. The anger from white Neshoba County residents regarding the outside scrutiny was instant and intense.

The first national reporters to interview Sheriff Rainey and Deputy Sheriff Price on Monday, June 22, were highly regarded reporters Claude Sitton of the *New York Times* and Karl Fleming of *Newsweek*.

The *New York Times*'s first story on the case was published on June 23, 1964, by Claude Sitton: "3 in Rights Drive Reported Missing: Mississippi Campaign Heads Fear Foul Play — Inquiry by F.B.I. Is Ordered." In it, Sheriff Lawrence Rainey is quoted as essentially saying that the disappearance was a hoax: "If they're missing, they just hid somewhere, trying to get a lot of publicity out of it, I figure."

When Sitton and Fleming were threatened with violence if they didn't leave town, the two reporters went inside a store in Philadelphia's courthouse square and asked the elderly white storekeeper for assistance. After hearing the reporters out, the man replied, "If you were a nigger and they were out there in the street beating you to death, I don't expect I'd go out and give them a hand, but they're absolutely right. If the nigger lovers and outside agitators would stay out of here and leave us alone, there wouldn't be any trouble. The best thing for you to do is what they say."

Stanley Dearman, a reporter for the *Meridian Star*, was one of many reporters assigned to work on the breaking story. He had seen Mickey Schwerner and James Chaney around Meridian but never talked to them. Etched in his memory is the last time he saw the two young men "walking very fast, going toward the post office. It wasn't long after that they disappeared." Now he was one of many reporters covering what was rapidly evolving from a local story into one of the hottest news stories in the nation.

Dearman arrived at the newspaper at 6:00 a.m. on the morning of Monday, June 22, 1964. His managing editor told him that "Schwerner and those boys didn't get back from Neshoba County last night." The editor said that it looked like something had happened to them and he told Dearman "to get the story." Dearman got in his car, drove to Philadelphia, and went to the courthouse. Sheriff Rainey was out, but his deputy sheriff, Cecil Price, was available. "And he told me they were held on a speeding charge and were held because they couldn't find the justice of the peace who had to set the bond. But what he was doing was just holding them till the Klan could organize and intercept them. He was very smooth. He had it down pat." Dearman believed that Price was lying. "You can tell when somebody is not telling you the whole story." Dearman would interview Price over a period of several months, and he gave the reporter an uneasy feeling. "Cecil Price gave me the creeps." Dearman felt that Price, "under the right circumstances, would have been a very cruel person."

The enormous attention on the missing men was not confined to the press. President Lyndon Johnson, who was working to get the 1964 Civil Rights Act passed by Congress, was focused on the case as well. On the afternoon of Tuesday, June 23, President Johnson was on the phone with Nicholas Katzenbach, the deputy attorney general. Johnson asked him what he thought happened to the three. Katzenbach replied, "I think they got picked up by some of these Klan people, be my guess." "And murdered?" Johnson asked. "Yeah, probably, or else they're just being hidden in one of those barns or something, you know, and getting the hell scared out of them," Katzenbach responded. "But I would not be surprised if they'd been murdered, Mr. President. Pretty rough characters."

In a conversation later that same afternoon with the president, Mississippi senator James Eastland stated that he didn't believe the three were missing and that their disappearance was simply a publicity stunt. As chairman of the

Senate Judiciary Committee, James Eastland was responsible for oversight of the Justice Department and the FBI. But Eastland and FBI Director J. Edgar Hoover developed a close relationship that allowed Hoover a free hand to generally do as he wished. The two men shared a dislike of radicals and a strong support for segregation. Eastland told the president, "Now, I'm going to tell you why I don't think there's a damn thing to it. They were put in jail in Philadelphia. . . . There's not a Ku Klux Klan in that area; there's not a Citizens' Council in that area; there's no organized white man in that area; so that's why I think it's a publicity stunt." Eastland later asked, "Who would . . . could possibly harm them?" Yet Neshoba County was well-known as being particularly hostile to the civil rights movement.

Eastland's view that the disappearance of the three men was nothing more than "a publicity stunt" was challenged moments later when President Johnson received a phone call from FBI Director Hoover that the men's burned-out vehicle was found near the Bogue

James Eastland (left) and Robert Kennedy in January 1961

Chitto swamp about eight miles northeast of Philadelphia. At the time of Hoover's call, bureau agents hadn't been able to get into the car, because of the intense heat, to determine whether any bodies were inside. But Hoover's conjecture was that "[t]hese men have been killed." In response, Johnson suggested the possibility that the men might have been kidnapped and "locked up" somewhere. The FBI director was skeptical. Hoover replied, "Well, I would doubt whether those people down there would even give them that much of a break."

Late that same afternoon on June 23, President Johnson was again talking to Hoover about the Mississippi crisis when he summoned into his office some of the family members

FBI Director J. Edgar Hoover *(left)* arrives in Jackson, Mississippi, on July 10, 1964. He is met by Jackson Mayor Allen Thompson.

of the missing men: Andy's parents, Robert and Carolyn Goodman; their attorney, Martin Popper; their congressman, Democrat William Ryan; Mickey's father, Nathan Schwerner; and his congressman, Republican Ogden Reid. As Johnson talked on the phone to Hoover, the visitors heard, presumably for the first time, that their sons' vehicle had been found — but there was still no news about whether their bodies were found in the burned-out hulk. The family members remained in the office while Johnson talked on the telephone to Secretary of Defense Robert McNamara about obtaining manpower assistance from the military in the search for the missing men.

That evening, the president received word that no bodies had been found in the car. Johnson telephoned Andy's father, who had already returned to New York City from his visit to Washington earlier in the day, as well as Mickey's mother in Pelham, New York, who did not come down to Washington with her husband. Johnson told them that more agents were being sent to the area to join in the search. He also told Anne Schwerner that the fact there were no bodies found in the car represented "a little hope that we didn't have earlier, and I thought that we would enjoy it as long as we could."

President Johnson continued to receive updates on the Mississippi case. In a conversation with Hoover the next day, on June 24, President Johnson asked, "That sheriff's [Lawrence Rainey's] a pretty bad fellow down there, isn't he?" Hoover responded, "Yes, he is. . . ." In the days and weeks to come, military personnel were enlisted in the effort

FBI agents and local law enforcement officers search the snake-infested Bogue Chitto swamp for clues regarding the missing three men.

Local youths mocking the search for the three civil rights workers

to find the missing men, and the FBI increased its presence in the state. The search for the men had been expanded to the Pearl River, located north of Philadelphia. The FBI had been spearheading the effort to drag the river for remains. The FBI's name for the case was Mississippi Burning, or "MIBURN" for short.

On June 25, President Johnson authorized the deployment of two hundred unarmed naval personnel to assist in the search for the three men. In response, Mississippi Democrat John Bell Williams took to the floor of the US House of Representatives to denounce the action, stating that President Johnson "surrendered" to the demand of "every left-wing agitator" in the nation.

Rita had left Oxford to travel to Mississippi. Veteran civil rights worker Bob Zellner, who had experience in the South, was dispatched to travel with her. They were at the Cincinnati airport waiting for their flight to Meridian when reporters came upon her to tell her that the vehicle had been found in Neshoba County. Fannie Lou Hamer, the woman who was beaten at the Winona bus station, was also at the airport. She drew Rita into her arms and the two of them wept. "Our tears were mingling with each other," Rita recalled.

Rita was unsuccessful in her attempt to meet with Mississippi's new governor, Paul B. Johnson Jr., an avowed segregationist who was known for routinely stating in his campaign speeches that "NAACP" stood for "niggers, apes, alligators, coons, and possums." However, she was successful in meeting with retired Director of Central Intelligence

Allen Dulles, who had been dispatched as President Johnson's emissary to the governor of Mississippi on this matter. FBI Director Hoover had always seen the Central Intelligence Agency (CIA) and the rest of the intelligence community as a threat to the FBI's power and jurisdiction. While Dulles was sensitive to Hoover's concerns, Johnson's selection of Dulles as an emissary to Mississippi was an implicit criticism of the FBI, and Hoover became anxious to show results in his investigation. Nevertheless, Dulles's meeting with Rita was brief. At the conclusion of the meeting, Dulles extended his sympathy. Rita replied, "I'm sorry. I don't need sympathy. I want my husband."

The burned-out vehicle used by the civil rights workers was found off Highway 21.

Rita was also determined to confront Sheriff Rainey and see the station wagon. When Rita, Bob Zellner, and a lawyer arrived at the Philadelphia motel where the FBI had set up shop, Rainey, accompanied by a state highway patrol investigator, approached Rita in the motel's parking lot. The sheriff, towering over Rita, exclaimed, "What in the goddamn hell are you doin' here?" Rita replied that she wanted to see her husband's vehicle, while the parking lot filled up with a posse of pickup trucks. He advised her to leave Neshoba County immediately. "I'm not leaving until I see Mickey's car," Rita responded, "and I don't care how many pickup trucks show up to intimidate me." The state highway official explained that Sheriff Rainey was in Meridian at his sick wife's bedside when Mickey and the others were arrested in Philadelphia and didn't know what had become of the men. Rita was not satisfied with that explanation. "I'm not leaving here until I learn what happened to my husband," Rita insisted. She pointedly told Rainey, "I'm going to keep drawing attention here until I find out, and if you don't like it you'll just have to have me killed, too." At that, Rainey flushed and his fist clenched. "I'm very shocked," he replied. "I'm sorry you said that."

Rainey told Rita and her companions that they could see the vehicle for five minutes, and then they had to leave the county. As Rita walked into the body shop, several of the white mechanics realized who she was and they laughed and let out rebel yells. After Rita and Zellner were shown the burned-out hulk, they left. As they drove away from Philadelphia,

Rita Schwerner *(center)* leaves the body shop where the station wagon was stored, as Sheriff Rainey looks on.

Rita's car was pelted with rocks and bottles and they were almost driven off the road by other vehicles.

Unlike the Goodmans and Schwerners, Fannie Lee Chaney didn't have supportive government officials in her state and local community pushing Mississippi and federal officials to find her son and bring to justice the individuals responsible for his disappearance. During that long summer of waiting, Julia Chaney noted that "not even the local government acknowledged my mother." However, the local government did acknowledge the Schwerner and Goodman families, but only to chide them for raising agitators who should have been kept at home. Julia recalls that not only did the state and local officials in Mississippi fail to offer any assistance, or even sympathy, to the Chaney family, but also that some of the family's relatives had distanced themselves "because they too had concerns for their own well-being and their families. Some friends and neighbors had distanced themselves as well." In addition, some of the church elders met and advised James's mother that she needed to move because she was "bringing risk to the entire neighborhood."

Fannie Lee Chaney had been finding it difficult to get work from white people since her oldest son had taken up the civil rights cause. She was making quilts to help feed her family. While waiting for word about her son, she spent a great deal of her time walking "from window to door, from room to room, crying and praying, and crying and praying." She often cleaned the house incessantly, sometimes four or five times a day.

The summer was particularly hard for young Ben Chaney. While he was anxious about his brother's fate, Ben was convinced that J.E. would somehow survive. "I think that my mother believed that my brother and the others were dead. I think she believed that because she's been there longer and that was the way of life with her. I think my sisters believed that they were dead. But I can pretty much say that until the funeral, I didn't think so. I just knew my brother. I knew that he would find a way to come through. He always came through. And I just knew that if there was any way for him to come through, he would be driving up the driveway in the morning. No doubt about it." To Ben, it was unthinkable that James wouldn't come home. "I was sure he'd be found, because I admired him so much, I looked up to him so much. He had all the right moves, he got all the girls. He was my big brother. And I guess I didn't believe he was dead until I saw him buried in the ground."

The Chaneys were also surprised to learn that summer that James had become a father. He had told his family about Mary Nan McCoy, a young woman he'd been seeing, and that he planned to marry her after Freedom Summer. Julia Chaney said that "he had told us of her, but we did not know that she was pregnant. I don't even know if he knew. He never saw his child." James's daughter, Angela, was born on June 11, 1964.

On June 29, Rita and Congressman Ogden Reid met with President Johnson and his civil rights assistant, Lee White, for approximately five minutes. Rita wanted to talk to the president about expanding the investigation. After the meeting, the president talked to Hoover about the encounter, which had upset the president. The president informed Hoover that he had met with Rita, who "wants thousands of extra people put down there and said I'm the only one that has the authority to do it. I told her I put all that we could efficiently handle, and I was going to let you determine how many we could efficiently handle. Now, I talked to McNamara this afternoon. He said he's got plenty of airmen and plenty [of] Army people in Mississippi, without moving them in, and plenty of Navy people." Hoover told the president during this same conversation that he planned to open a permanent bureau office in Jackson, Mississippi, and would send up to four hundred additional agents to supplement the two hundred FBI agents he claimed were already in the state.

After her meeting with President Johnson, Rita told the press that she had appealed to the president to assign five thousand men to the search. She criticized the president for arguing that "nowhere near thousands of men" could be used in the search while simultaneously arguing that the federal government was doing everything in its power to conduct the search.

FBI investigators had a difficult time eliciting leads from the people of Neshoba County, who were defensive and hostile to the outsiders who had swarmed over their homeland. A reporter for *Life* magazine summed up his perception of Philadelphia, Mississippi, at the end of 1964:

> This is a strange, tight little town. Its fear and hatred of things that come from the outside is nearly pathological. As the stranger walks its streets, hostile eyes track him as a swivel gun tracks a target. Yet it is quiet and there is even a certain uniform sense of self-contentment in its conviction that all its troubles are caused by outsiders — by reporters; by militant, uppity Negroes; by the federal government. Philadelphia is barely willing to admit that an inhuman crime did take place, and it is quite unable to feel any collective guilt. It is, in short, a town which has deluded itself endlessly and which is still doing so.

On July 24, 1964, Dr. Martin Luther King Jr., accompanied by Andrew Young, Ralph Abernathy, John Lewis, and other civil rights activists, visited Neshoba County. When he visited Philadelphia, Dr. King told a group gathered at a local pool hall that he had no doubt that the three missing men who had been held at the local jail down the street had been murdered and that blacks in the local community lived with fear. "But if we are gonna be free as a people we've got to shed ourselves of fear, and we've got to say to those who oppose us with violence that you can't stop us by bombing a

In July 1964, while still recovering
from the injuries he sustained by the
KKK, Bud Cole (right) welcomes Martin
Luther King Jr. to his farm.

church," he stated. "You can't stop us by shooting at us. You can't stop us by brutalizing us, because we're gonna keep on keeping on until we're free." The civil rights leader urged the black residents of Philadelphia to encourage their family and friends to register with the Mississippi Freedom Democratic Party. King's caravan drove out to the countryside to briefly visit the ruins of the Mount Zion Methodist Church. They then paid a visit to Bud and Beatrice Cole's farmhouse nearby to hear firsthand about their assault from the Klansmen.

For years, blacks in Neshoba County suffered the same indignities that blacks suffered elsewhere in Mississippi and

Martin Luther King Jr. talks to
Beatrice Cole at the Cole family farm.

throughout the South at that time. Jewel Rush grew up in Neshoba County, and her parents taught her how to act around white people: "Stay in your place; say 'Yes, ma'am' and 'No, ma'am.'" As the Rush family lived out in the country, Jewel normally wasn't around white people except when they came to town to buy clothing or go to the drugstore to get a cone of ice cream. "Usually, we would be the last to be waited on. We couldn't go in the restaurants and get anything because we weren't allowed." When she and her family came to the town of Philadelphia, they knew they must "stay close and pay attention, not do anything." Blacks could attend the Ellis Theater in Philadelphia, but they could only sit upstairs in the movie house. A lot of blacks wanted to vote, "but they couldn't get any place when [they] go to the courthouse."

Sheriff Lawrence Rainey and Deputy Sheriff Cecil Price enjoyed exercising their power over the black community in Neshoba County and were "like two peas in a pod." Rainey and Price were generally assumed to be members of the Ku Klux Klan. In 1963, Rainey was elected sheriff. He had run for the office of sheriff on a slogan of "Elect Rainey and Leave the Niggers and Nigger Lovers to Him." It was already well-known that Rainey had killed two black men while serving as a deputy.

Jewel Rush, who lived in the county outside Philadelphia, recalled that there was a community center in Philadelphia where the black residents would hold dances. It was not uncommon when a dance was being held for Rainey and Price to enter, with the apparent objective of intimidating the participants. "The music and everything would stop when they came in. And they'd just look; they had their flashlights and they would just look around and look around. And as soon as they walked out the door, the music would start again" and the dance would resume. Sheriff Rainey also imposed a curfew requiring blacks to be off the streets of Philadelphia by 10:00 p.m. If you were black, Sheriff Rainey and Deputy Price would "run you home." "They would chase you, put the spotlight on you, and make you run, and say 'Run, nigger, run!'" The whites, however, had no curfew and "could go anyplace" and "do anything."

The bullying behavior of Sheriff Rainey and Deputy Price not only intimidated the local black community but many in the white community as well. Jewel noted that many whites in the county were just as afraid of Rainey and Price. "They walked around with the big cowboy hats and the boots and the big guns on the side. . . . They just ruled everything." Sheriff Rainey was "just a person — and Price, too. I called them hoodlums. They were just doing stuff just to be doing it."

Not everyone in Neshoba County's white community supported the Jim Crow system of segregation. For example, Buford Posey, who was widely considered a local eccentric. After World War II, he became the first white person in Mississippi to join the NAACP. He would later argue that the black veterans of World War II should be able to vote in the nation they had fought to defend. Posey recalled immediately after the murders: "I received this phone call that said, 'We killed three of your friends tonight, and you're next.'" To Posey, the voice sounded like Edgar Ray Killen. "The Klan boasted openly. It was common knowledge. By God, if you weren't blind or hard of hearing, you knew it if you just go on the streets of Philadelphia." Posey told investigators that "I'd look to the sheriff's department if I was looking for the murderers. They said they placed little credence in what I said, but they turned around and indicted the same damn people I named at that time." When Posey's contact with investigators became known and he continued to be outspoken with the press regarding his views on the likely murderers, his life was threatened and he fled Neshoba County.

Another one of the few white citizens of Neshoba County who held dissenting views of the prevailing attitudes on race was Florence Mars, whose family had lived in the county for generations. Her grandfather owned a great deal of property in the area, and she often traveled with him and became acquainted with many black people. Stanley Dearman recalled that "Florence was something of a misfit, but I mean that in a good way. She didn't tow the party line. And she did her own thinking." And she had her own ideas about justice and racial equality. FBI agents investigating the murders had great difficulty in finding cooperative white citizens in Neshoba County to interview. Mars and her aunt Ellen Spendrup had no direct knowledge about the murders but provided the FBI with valuable background about the community. When the two women later gave testimony to a federal grand jury regarding Sheriff Rainey, threats against Mars increased.

The disappearance of the three men hung over Neshoba County, Freedom Summer, and the country during the summer of 1964. As July ended, it seemed increasingly unlikely that the three civil rights workers would be found alive. But by August, the long summer of uncertainty for the Chaney, Goodman, and Schwerner families — and the nation — was about to come to an end.

CHAPTER 6

THREE STREAKS OF LIGHTNING IN THE SKY

[W]hen people die on a cross, they sacrifice. That's what this was. This was a sacrifice of life that furthered the cause, and to get that you [have] got to get the force on the other side that's willing to kill. . . . You have got to find somebody that is willing to die and somebody that is willing to commit murder.

— Florence Mars

Many thought the men were dead as soon as they were reported missing. For one Mississippi boy, the disappearance was particularly heartfelt. Larry Martin spent a great deal of time at the community center with the Schwerners. Larry's grandmother had a little restaurant next to the beauty parlor where his mother worked. He would recall the investigators descending on the COFO office, trying to find out what happened to the three men. "The policemen and sheriffs were coming up, asking questions. All kinds of men with suits on, asking questions. The office was busy then. People were trying to find out what was going on. You heard so many stories. I think it was my grandmother [who] said she remembered a man come in to eat and said that when it started to rain, he saw three streaks of lightning in the sky. I never will forget that as long as I live. I thought it meant they were dead and buried."

The FBI worked throughout the summer to investigate what had become of the three missing men. An informant finally provided the information that the three were buried in an earthen dam at Olen Burrage's Old Jolly Farm. The dam was enormous: 20 feet high, 547 feet long, and 83 feet thick at the base. In all, it was estimated that approximately 27,000 cubic feet of earth had to be removed in order to exhume the bodies. A bulldozer and other excavation equipment were trucked to Neshoba County from Jackson in the early morning of Tuesday, August 4, the forty-fourth day since the civil rights workers had gone missing.

It was particularly hot on that summer day in Mississippi, with the temperature reaching more than 100 degrees. In midafternoon, the odor of decaying flesh was detectable by the workers, several of whom had been combat veterans and recognized the unmistakable smell. The stench was appalling.

When approximately fourteen feet of dirt had been removed, a pair of men's boots became visible and the bulldozer and excavation equipment were removed from the scene. The agents then resorted to using shovels and hand spades. Greenish-blue blowflies swarmed in a frenzy in the pit and buzzards circled overhead. Several additional hours of careful digging yielded the remains of three individuals. Identification on the bodies removed any doubt about the identity of the corpses.

As Andy's body was removed from the dam, the FBI agents noticed something unusual. The FBI report noted that "[t]he left hand of this body was clenched in a tight fist. Opening of this fist disclosed a rocklike object." This detail strongly suggests that Andy was still alive when the Klan dumped him in the burial pit. Ruth Grunzweig was horrified to learn this fact: "That was the worst."

August 4, 1964, was a tumultuous day for President Johnson. In addition to his many responsibilities, on this day he was dealing with a naval engagement between the United States and North Vietnamese forces at the Gulf of Tonkin, which would lead to the escalation of American involvement in the Vietnam War. Shortly after 8:00 p.m., President Johnson received a phone call at the White House from Assistant FBI Director Deke DeLoach. DeLoach told the president that the FBI had found three bodies six miles southwest from Philadelphia, Mississippi. Given the tremendous amount of press interest in the case, both men knew that this news would spread rapidly. Accordingly, the FBI wanted to announce it publicly, but the president told him to hold off for several minutes until the families could be notified. The president directed his staff to get word to the families before they learned about it from television or the radio. In a phone call from his civil rights assistant, Lee White, the president was informed that "I've already talked to Mrs. [Fannie Lee] Chaney, and I talked to Mrs. [Rita] Schwerner, the widow."

"Yeah," the president replied. "You talked to Schwerner and Chaney and who else?"

This photo of the three men was taken by the FBI soon after the bodies were uncovered in an earthen dam on Olen Burrage's Old Jolly Farm on August 4, 1964.

Lee White replied, "The Goodman family are out at the theater, but I got their son, an eighteen-year-old boy [David Goodman], and talked to him. And the Schwerners themselves, the parents of the boy who was missing, are traveling in Vermont. Their — I talked to their son [Steve Schwerner], and he said he didn't know how to get in touch with them, that they just left by automobile this morning, and he probably wouldn't know how to get them, but that they would call him."

Johnson asked their reaction to the news. White replied, "Well, the two young boys [David Goodman and Steve Schwerner] — both of them — and the widow [Rita Schwerner] also expected it. They were not at all surprised or shaken. Mrs. [Fannie Lee] Chaney, the Negro woman, sounded a little torn up a bit. I explained to her that we just weren't positive yet. . . ."

But in a short time that evening, it would be clear that the bodies were in fact Mickey, James, and Andy. The bodies were moved directly to the University of Mississippi Medical Center in Jackson. The FBI had specifically requested that Cecil Price, by now a suspect in the murder investigation, join in bringing the bodies from the burial site and had him attend the autopsy in Jackson to observe his reaction. But Price was impassive; the federal agents had seldom seen a more unflappable murder suspect.

Later that evening, DeLoach and President Johnson spoke again, and DeLoach mentioned that "[w]e have some excellent circumstantial evidence, but we don't have enough to cause any arrests right now." Johnson asked if the bureau had an informer who provided the location of the bodies, and DeLoach responded affirmatively, noting that it was "[s]omeone that we have to protect with a great deal of caution. . . ."

The lengthy autopsy showed that both Mickey and Andy had each been shot once in the chest area with no indication of broken bones. The autopsy revealed James's cause of death as being a gunshot wound to his head, with additional bullets removed from both his chest and abdomen. The pathologist indicated that "fractured and broken bones were present in the

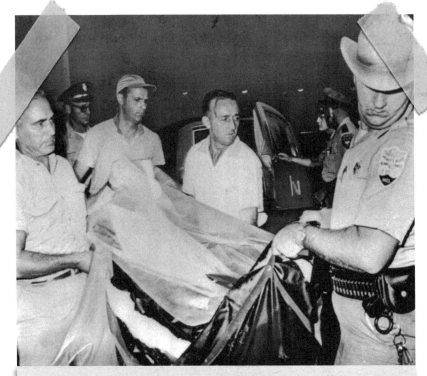

Deputy Sheriff Cecil Price *(right)* assists in unloading the bodies of the civil rights workers at the University of Mississippi Medical Center in Jackson so they can be autopsied.

jaw, upper limbs, and left shoulder" of James's body. Because of the advanced state of decomposition, the pathologist stated that "he could not reliably determine whether or not victim Chaney [was] beaten to any degree prior to shooting." It was suggested that James's broken bones "could have been produced by heavy bulldozer in burying or exhuming body."

Because of their suspicion of Mississippi officials, COFO arranged for New York pathologist Dr. David Spain to provide a second opinion regarding the cause of death of the three men. Ultimately, he only conducted an autopsy of James Chaney. In conducting the autopsy, he stated that "the lower jaw was completely shattered, split vertically, from some tremendous force. . . . I carefully examined the body, and found that the bones in the right shoulder were crushed — again, from some strong and direct blow." Spain noted that "one thing was certain: This frail boy had been beaten in an inhuman fashion. The blows that had so terribly shattered his bones — I surmised he must have been beaten with chains or a pipe — were in themselves sufficient to cause death." He noted that James's skull was crushed as well. In summary, he stated that "I could barely believe the destruction to these frail young bones. In my twenty-five years as a pathologist and medical examiner, I have never seen bones so severely shattered, except in tremendously high-speed accidents or airplane crashes. It was obvious to any first-year medical student that this boy had been beaten to a pulp."

The news media quickly spread word of the discovery of the bodies on the evening of August 4. Roscoe Jones recalled his reaction to the news in Meridian, where he was attending a concert at a local church with folk singer Pete Seeger: "Pete Seeger announced that the bodies had been found. I started crying."

In the summer of 1964, Ralph Engelman was working at a newspaper in Michigan. During the course of the summer, he sent a letter to Andy's parents, reflecting on his friendship with Andy but referring to Andy as if his friend's life was over. This was the first time Andy's mother had heard of her son being referred to in the past tense, and it upset her. But the harsh truth came to Carolyn on the evening of August 4, when she and Bobby joined with friends to see a mime troupe perform at Lincoln Center. It was the first time the couple had gone out socially since Andy had disappeared. Their son went missing on Father's Day, and August 5 was Bobby's fiftieth birthday. During the performance, a family friend appeared in the aisle, urgently motioning to Bobby so he could give the news that the Goodmans had been waiting for as well as dreading.

Jane Mark had been at camp at Tupper Lake for the summer. Andy Goodman was well-known at this camp, and Jane remembers the summer

Roscoe Jones, who, as a teenager, worked with Mickey and James

as being horrible, waiting for news about her cousin. When the bodies were discovered, Jane's mother telephoned her at the camp that evening to tell her the news. "I was by myself and went screaming down this road." It was one thing to know in her heart that Andy was dead, "it's another thing to actually have somebody confirm that for you." Jane's parents came and took their distraught daughter home.

The day after the three bodies were discovered, President Johnson called FBI Director Hoover to congratulate him and the FBI on their work on the case. Hoover replied, "We have the names of the people who did it. In order to prove it, it's going to be a little tougher job. The sheriff [Lawrence Rainey] was in on it. The deputy sheriff [Cecil Price] was in on it. The justice of the peace was in on it. And there were seven other men. We have all those names, and as they say, we're concentrating now on developing the evidence. We're going to call a grand jury in possibly the next two weeks, concerning the burning of the church, and bring before the grand jury these . . . particular ten men, hoping that one of them may then break." Hoover also indicated that the Ku Klux Klan was behind the murders.

James was the first to be buried. Shortly after his body was released from the University of Mississippi Medical Center in Jackson in the early evening of Friday, August 7, 1964, James was laid to rest at Okatibbee Cemetery, a black cemetery outside of Meridian. Only the immediate family and a handful of close friends were present. James's younger brother, Ben, was particularly distraught and cried out, "I want my brother! I want my brother!" There was a memorial service later that evening at the First Union Baptist Church in Meridian, attended by hundreds. Roscoe Jones recalled Meridian being "bombarded with people" in the wake of the discovery of the bodies. He didn't have any desire to go to James's funeral. It was too painful. "I wanted to forget it."

Among the eulogies given at James Chaney's memorial service was one from Dave Dennis, CORE's senior representative in Mississippi. He had been asked to be low-kcy and reassuring

Ben Chaney is comforted during the memorial service for his brother.

in his remarks. But as he stepped up to the podium and saw young Ben Chaney weeping, he snapped. "So I just stopped and said what I felt. There was no need to stand in front of that kid, Ben Chaney, and lie to him." Dennis said to the mourners:

> . . . You see, I know what is going to happen. I feel it deep in my heart — when they find the people who killed those guys in Neshoba County . . . they [will] come back to the state of Mississippi and have a jury of all their cousins and aunts and uncles. And I know what they are going to say: "Not guilty." Because no one saw them pull the trigger.

Andy's funeral was held two days later at the Society for Ethical Culture's meeting house in his Upper West Side neighborhood. When Carolyn came into the hall, she later recalled being startled to see her middle son. "I walked into the memorial and I saw him, five years old, dressed up to perform for the family, sitting on top of the

Carolyn Goodman overwhelmed upon seeing her son's casket.

coffin, which of course, was closed. He had been buried for forty-four days. But there he was. I still see him there, even today."

Among the eulogies offered was one by Andy's close friend Ralph Engelman. He noted that "[o]n the eve of his departure for Oxford, Ohio, Andy not only was conscious of the danger which awaited him but also spoke with equal concern about the special risk being taken by Mississippi Negroes who would remain when the Summer Project was over. . . . In going to Mississippi, Andy risked not only death but dying in vain."

At the conclusion of Andy's memorial service, Carolyn Goodman linked arms with Fannie Lee Chaney, who had come to New York right after her own son's funeral, and Anne Schwerner. They walked out to the street, where hundreds of people were paying their respects and softly singing "We Shall Overcome." Andy's cousin Jane Mark walked outside, and her reaction to seeing the large crowd was one of anger. Who were these strangers making a claim on her cousin? "I remember coming outside and looking around and saying, this is my cousin. He's my brother. What are all you strangers doing here? You didn't know him. He's not your dead cousin." Jane had a difficult time dealing with Andy's death. "I would have nightmares of what Andy must have felt like being shot — I mean really visual kind of images of what it would be like."

The Schwerners attempted to have Mickey buried next to his friend James Chaney in a black cemetery, but segregation

The mothers of the three slain men, *(from left)* Fannie Lee Chaney, Carolyn Goodman, and Anne Schwerner, walk out onto 64th Street in New York City after Andy Goodman's funeral.

Rita Schwerner *(foreground)*, along with Mickey's parents, Nathan and Anne Schwerner, leave Mickey's memorial service.

extended to Mississippi's graveyards. No white undertaker was willing to assist with such a plan, and the black undertaker handling James Chaney's funeral was afraid of retribution if he assisted in handling a white man's remains. Mickey's body was transported to New York, where it was cremated.

Right after Andy's funeral, Mickey's memorial service was held at the Community Church in New York City. In his eulogy, attorney and family friend William Kunstler stated:

Beyond the immediacy of our grief, every one of us feels, in one way or another, that we can look to tomorrow with brighter and clearer eyes, that we can face the morning sun with more faith and courage, that we are stronger and more resolute than ever before because our three friends laid down their lives in the dark of a Mississippi night. We are not afraid because they were not afraid — we will walk hand in hand because they walked hand in hand — we will live together because they died together.

The fact that others were dying in the fight against segregation, but without public awareness, was underscored to Steve Schwerner in a conversation he had with black civil rights activist Stokely Carmichael at Mickey's memorial service. Carmichael indicated that this was the seventeenth funeral he'd been to, and all of the deceased had been black and from Mississippi, but "nobody knows about" them. This insight was also noted by another civil rights activist. Two days after the bodies were found, Ella Baker, executive director of the Washington office of the Mississippi Freedom Democratic Party, spoke at the organization's convention in Jackson, Mississippi. "The tragedy has become a symbol," she said. "The unfortunate thing is that it took this kind of symbol to make the rest of the country turn its eyes on the fact that there are other bodies lying under the swamps of Mississippi. Until the killing of a black mother's son becomes as important as the killing of a white mother's son, we who believe in freedom cannot rest."

Young Ben Chaney was experiencing anger along with

grief. On August 16, 1964, two months after Mount Zion Methodist Church was burned to the ground, a memorial service was held for the three civil rights martyrs at the charred rubble where the church once stood in Longdale. While the service was held, Sheriff Rainey and Deputy Sheriff Price stood apart and observed. Eleven-year-old Ben made a speech, and he concluded his remarks defiantly proclaiming: "And I want us all to stand up here together and say just one thing. I want the sheriff to hear this good. *We ain't scared no more of Sheriff Rainey!*" Ben recalled, "After I made that speech, my father gave me a hard time. He was talking, 'Forget it. Let bygones be bygones.' I guess he was saying mercy, or forgiveness, and all that stuff. What I remember most is how sad the whole affair was. Throughout the funeral and the memorial service, I kept wondering why didn't people do something. Why didn't my father, my grandfather, my great-grandfather? Why wasn't things made different? Why wasn't change taking place then, so that this event wouldn't be taking place now? I felt a desire to do something to hurt the people that hurt my brother. At that time I couldn't do anything."

As the three men were laid to rest, the FBI continued its investigation into the murders and Freedom Summer was winding down, but the memory of the young men and their sacrifice endured. When Martin Luther King Jr. gave his acceptance speech for receiving the Nobel Peace Prize in Oslo, Norway, on December 10, 1964, he noted that "in

Philadelphia, Mississippi, young people seeking to secure the right to vote were brutalized and murdered." By the end of 1964, the federal government was coming closer to making its case against those responsible for the murders. Yet the road to justice would prove to be a long one.

Dr. Martin Luther King Jr. speaks to members of the Mississippi Freedom Democratic Party (MFDP) and demonstrators on the Atlantic City boardwalk during the August 1964 Democratic National Convention. Behind him are images of the three slain civil rights workers.

Neshoba County juries rarely convicted a white man of murder, and white men almost never went to the penitentiary for murder. We had a saying that "if you want to kill somebody, Neshoba County is the place to do it."
— Florence Mars

After the FBI's extensive investigation into the triple murders, the Justice Department began preparations to present its evidence to a grand jury at the end of 1964. But should the case be prosecuted by federal authorities or the state?

Unless committed on federal property, murder is a violation of state law rather than federal law. Mississippi's state officials, even if they had an interest in prosecuting the case, knew it would be highly unpopular to prosecute individuals for a crime against perceived agitators seeking to undermine Mississippi's segregationist way of life. If the state were to go forward with a prosecution, it would have to bring the case to Neshoba County, where the crime occurred. This course of action seemed unrealistic, as the information being gathered by the FBI implicated officials in local law enforcement.

After continued discussions with the state, federal officials decided to go forward and present evidence to a federal grand jury under federal statutes that apply against individuals who have deprived others of their civil rights.

On December 4, 1964, four months to the day after the bodies of James Chaney, Andrew Goodman, and Michael Schwerner were found, federal agents fanned out to arrest twenty-one individuals for conspiring to deny the three murdered men of their civil rights. The arrests had been expected, and none of the suspects resisted arrest.

On December 10, the accused men were brought before Esther Carter, the US Commissioner for the Southern District

On December 10, 1964, defendants stand before Esther Carter *(seated)* for a preliminary hearing regarding their roles in the Freedom Summer murder case.

of Mississippi, for a preliminary hearing to rule on the government being able to send the case before a grand jury. To the surprise of federal authorities, Carter, who was not a lawyer, ruled that Horace Doyle Barnette's signed confession was hearsay evidence because only one individual, an FBI agent, heard the confession from Barnette. Carter would not change her mind, and the Justice Department withdrew from the hearing rather than reveal more of the federal case. Carter dismissed all charges against the defendants. The defendants were jubilant as they left the hearing room. The federal prosecutors and civil rights activists present, including Fannie Lee Chaney, were furious.

In January 1965, the Department of Justice asked US District Judge Harold Cox, a close friend of the segregationist senator James Eastland and famously hostile to blacks and the civil rights movement, to convene a grand jury. The federal grand jury ultimately indicted eighteen of the men. However, on February 24, 1965, Cox dismissed the felony charges against all of the defendants except James Jordan, whose case had been transferred to Georgia. The matter was appealed to the US Supreme Court, which handed down its unanimous ruling on March 28, 1966, in *United States v. Price* (1966), reversing Judge Cox's ruling and clearing the way for the federal trial to proceed.

During this time, Neshoba County remained a closed, insular society, determined to retain the racial status quo and mistrustful and resentful of outside influence. This attitude was still evident two years after the infamous triple murder.

Martin Luther King Jr.'s second visit to Neshoba County was far more tumultuous than his first visit the month after the three civil rights workers disappeared. On June 21, 1966, King and Ralph Abernathy went to Philadelphia, Mississippi, along with twenty volunteers, to commemorate the two-year

In January 1966, a man holds a photo of Cecil Price and Lawrence Rainey laughing at their arraignment with the ironic title "Support Your Local Police."

anniversary of the murders of J.E., Andy, and Mickey. Dr. King led a march of several hundred local black people from Mount Nebo Baptist Church on the outskirts of Philadelphia to the courthouse in the center of town.

As they marched up Beacon Street Hill to the courthouse square, local whites jeered at them and screamed obscenities. When some of the whites recognized black marchers, they became enraged. White motorists buzzed the marchers in their vehicles and raced their engines when they got to the courthouse square to drown out the marchers' prayers.

Young Dick Molpus had been admonished by his mother not to go into town that day "because there's going to be trouble." So naturally, "I ran right up there," he recalled. He went to the courthouse square, where the old-fashioned sidewalks were elevated high above the streets. As Dr. King and the marchers came to the town square amid a furious white mob, Dick looked over to see Florence Mars, the town eccentric on racial matters, "holding an American flag, welcoming Dr. King." He never forgot that moment; it "had a profound impact on me. I had just seen an act of conscience and courage."

Encountering Deputy Sheriff Cecil Price, King addressed the crowd, "In this county, Andrew Goodman, James Chaney, and Mickey Schwerner were brutally murdered," he cried. "I believe in my heart that the murderers are somewhere around me at this moment."

A voice close to Cecil Price replied, "You damn right, they're right behind you."

King continued, "They ought to search their hearts. I want them to know that we are not afraid. If they kill three of us, they will have to kill all of us." As the marchers applauded, King stated, "I am not afraid of any man, whether he is in Mississippi or Michigan, whether he is in Birmingham or Boston. I am not afraid of any man."

Someone in the crowd yelled at King, "Hey, Luther! Thought you wasn't scared of anybody. Come up here alone and prove it!" At that moment, a string of explosions like

On the two-year anniversary of the Freedom Summer murders, Martin Luther King Jr. led a march in honor of the three civil rights workers to Philadelphia, Mississippi. Deputy Sheriff Cecil Price *(left)* halts the march at the Neshoba County Courthouse.

machine gunfire were heard. It turned out to be a string of firecrackers.

As King led the marchers out of town, the confrontation burst into violence with several whites striking out against the marchers with their fists and throwing bottles, stones, clubs, and firecrackers. Only when black youths started fighting back did the police intervene in the melee to restore order. When the violence subsided, King told a reporter, "This is a terrible town, the worst I've seen. There is a complete reign of terror here."

After additional procedural delays, a new grand jury reindicted the conspirators on February 28, 1967. There were several changes to the defendant list. Earl Akin, Tommy Horne, and Oliver Warner were dropped from the list because they were alleged to have known about the plot without having necessarily participated in it. Another two were dropped because of their age: teenager Jimmy Lee Townsend and the elderly Otha Burkes. Three names were added to the list of defendants: the Imperial Wizard of the White Knights of the Ku Klux Klan in Mississippi, Sam Bowers; Philadelphia police officer Richard Willis; and former Neshoba sheriff Ethel Glen "Hop" Barnett.

At last, the federal trial began in Meridian, Mississippi, on October 9, 1967, with Judge Cox presiding. The prosecution was led by John Doar, head of the Justice Department's civil rights division. There were a dozen attorneys from Neshoba County and Lauderdale County handling the defense. The defense was undoubtedly hopeful that Cox would be inclined to be more supportive of the defense than the federal prosecutors. They were dispelled of that notion early in the trial.

Reverend Charles Johnson, a black minister, was on the stand for the prosecution to provide background and describe Mickey Schwerner's activities in early 1964. Under cross-examination, a defense attorney asked whether Mickey Schwerner was an atheist. He also asked Reverend Johnson if he "and Mr. Schwerner didn't advocate and try to get young male Negroes to sign statements agreeing to rape a white woman once a week during the hot summer of 1964?" The judge declared the question "highly improper" and demanded to see some basis for the question to be asked. When the defense attorney stated that the question was passed to him to ask, the judge demanded, "Well, who is the author of that question?" Another defense attorney finally responded, "Brother [Edgar Ray] Killen wrote the question, one of the defendants." An angry Judge Cox replied: "I'm not going to allow a farce to be made of this trial and everybody might as well get that through their heads, including every one of these defendants right now. . . . I don't understand such a question as that, and I don't appreciate it."

Testimony in the trial shed more light on the nature and extent of the Klan's plot to murder Mickey Schwerner. For instance, Meridian policeman Sergeant Carlton Wallace Miller testified that he was recruited into the Ku Klux Klan by Edgar Ray Killen and that many of his codefendants were either members of the Klan or among those present at Klan meetings. James Jordan testified about his role in the killings of the three men, and Reverend Delmar Dennis testified that Ku Klux Klan Imperial Wizard Sam Bowers indicated he was "pleased" after the murders.

On October 18, John Doar made the closing argument for the federal government, summarizing at length the facts of the case. "Members of the jury, this is an important case. It is important to the government. It's important to the defendants, but most important, it's important to the state of Mississippi." Echoing President Abraham Lincoln's Gettysburg Address, Doar continued, "What I say, what the other lawyers say here today, what the court says about the law will soon be forgotten, but what you twelve people do here today will long be remembered." He concluded by saying that "[i]f you find that these men are not guilty you will declare the law of Neshoba County to be the law of the state of Mississippi."

Later that day, Judge Cox directed the jury to begin deliberations on the case. One day later, the jury reported that it was unable to render a verdict. However, the judge directed the jury to resume deliberations in what is known as an "Allen charge" or "dynamite charge" to encourage a deadlocked jury to come to a verdict. During a subsequent recess, defendant Wayne Roberts was overheard joking with Cecil Price that "Judge Cox just gave that jury a 'dynamite charge.' We've got some dynamite for them ourselves." This comment was reported back to Judge Cox, who was not amused.

Finally, on the morning of October 20, the jury announced it had reached unanimous verdicts on all but three of the defendants. The clerk read: "We, the jury, find the defendant Cecil Ray Price not guilty." Veteran journalist Bill Minor of the New Orleans *Times-Picayune* was present and he noted "a sigh came from a woman in the crowd believed to be Price's wife." The clerk quickly corrected herself and continued, "I'm sorry, Your Honor, may I start over? . . . We, the jury, find the defendant Cecil Ray Price guilty of the charges contained in the indictment." Minor reported that "Price's wife put her hand to her throat and uttered a gasp, as tension grew in the partly filled courtroom." In addition to Cecil Price and Jimmy Arledge, the jury found Sam Bowers, Alton Wayne Roberts, Jimmie Snowden, Billy Wayne Posey, and Horace Doyle Barnette guilty. The jury wasn't able to come to a verdict regarding Edgar Ray Killen, Jerry McGrew Sharpe, and E. G. "Hop" Barnett. The jury found Lawrence Rainey, Herman Tucker, and Olen Burrage not guilty. After the verdicts were read, Cox

Edgar Ray Killen *(left)* and Cecil Price casually await their verdicts.

dismissed everyone except Price and Roberts and had them approach the bench to rebuke them for their "joke" about the dynamite charge. He denied them bond and had them jailed over the weekend.

The convicted defendants were sentenced by Judge Cox on December 29. Bowers and Roberts were sentenced to ten years in prison, and Posey and Price received six years. Arledge, Snowden, and Barnette each received three years. James Jordan was tried in federal court in Atlanta, where he pleaded no contest to conspiracy charges and was sentenced to four years. Judge Cox later stated that "[t]hey killed one nigger, one Jew, and a white man. I gave them all what I thought they deserved." After a series of appeals, the seven men entered federal custody on March 19, 1970.

The convicted men served time in prison (all were paroled before serving their full prison sentences), returned to their communities, and lived out their lives. In 1999, Alton Wayne Roberts died of heart trouble. Lawrence Rainey, who was acquitted in the case, would never again have the power he wielded in Neshoba County as

James Jordan is surrounded by FBI agents as he leaves the federal courthouse.

sheriff. Rainey went on to work as an automobile mechanic and as a security guard for a shopping mall in Meridian. Rainey's involvement in the events of June 21, 1964, would follow him for the rest of his life. He died of cancer in November 2002, at the age of seventy-nine. As Rainey would later state, "If nobody had paid those boys any mind, they'd have come and gone and they wouldn't have meant a thing . . . nothing, nothing at all."

CHAPTER 8
MISSISSIPPI MOVES TOWARD A MURDER TRIAL

I believed at the time, and I continue to believe today, that if all three of the men killed in Neshoba County had been black, the nation would have taken little notice. This is a society which values white lives more.

— Rita Schwerner Bender, Comments Upon the Twenty-Fifth Anniversary Commemoration at Statuary Hall, US Congress, June 23, 1989

After the tumultuous summer of 1964, the families of the three victims tried to move on with their lives.

Life in Meridian became increasingly difficult for the Chaney family after James's murder, as local whites would not leave them alone. Fannie Lee stated that "[t]hey kept shooting at my house, and once they tried to throw a bomb. I was scared to send Ben to school." James's gravesite was also vandalized. Fannie Lee was not able to find a job. In 1965, with the assistance of the Goodman family and the Schwerner family, Fannie Lee, Ben, and his sister Janice moved from Mississippi to New York. Fannie Lee found a job as a nurse's aide at a nursing home. Julia Chaney would later move up to the New York City area and seldom returned to Mississippi.

Ben Chaney was the first recipient of a scholarship from the Andrew Goodman Foundation and attended the Walden School. He also traveled with his mother and spoke extensively on civil rights, with some even suggesting that he might become the first black president of the United States. His sister Julia said at the time that "James's death really did affect him. So much was forced on him . . . people telling him, 'You've gotta live up to James.' He was just exposed to too much. Everybody seemed to have a stake in him, and after a while, he came to see that he wasn't fulfilling his own dreams." Ben's interest in the Walden School waned, and he began spending time with black militants. In 1970, just shy of his eighteenth birthday, Ben and two other young men traveled to Florida. The trip turned into a criminal rampage in which four white people were shot to death. Ben was not accused of pulling the trigger, but ultimately was convicted of first-degree murder and served thirteen years in prison for crimes he said he didn't commit. When he left prison, he went to work for former US Attorney General Ramsey Clark and established the James Earl Chaney Foundation.

On June 20, 1965, the Goodmans held a ceremony at Andy's gravesite unveiling a memorial sculpture at Mount Judah Cemetery in Queens. The sculpture depicts outstretched arms and contains a quote from the poet Stephen Spender: "He travelled a short while towards the sun and left the vivid air signed by his honour." The folk group Peter, Paul and Mary performed the song "Blowin' in the Wind" at the ceremony, one of Andy's favorite songs.

With the death of their son, Robert and Carolyn Goodman created the Andrew Goodman Foundation in 1966 to perpetuate the purpose and spirit of Andy's life. Carolyn would run the foundation for the rest of her life. Andy's father, Robert, died of a stroke in 1969 at the age of fifty-four. He was heartbroken at Andy's death, and some believe this tragedy contributed to Bobby's own early death. Carolyn remarried, and would later be widowed a second time after twenty years of marriage. She continued to live in the family's spacious Upper West Side apartment in New York City, where

At the dedication of a memorial to Andrew Goodman at the Walden School in 1965 are *(left to right)* James Chaney's sister Barbara; Ben Chaney Jr.; Andy's parents, Carolyn and Robert Goodman; Andy's brothers, Jonathan and David; and Andy's first cousin Amy Goodman.

she converted Andy's bedroom into an office, continued her social activism, and kept her son's memory alive.

Mickey's parents, Anne and Nathan Schwerner, went on to raise funds for organizations such as CORE and SNCC and lobbied for federal voting rights legislation. In the year after Mickey was murdered, Nathan Schwerner estimated that he had spoken to between fifty and sixty organizations. "I felt very early that I had the alternative of merely succumbing to grief or trying to do something about the situation. So I decided to do what I could to advance the things Mickey and I both believed in." Nathan Schwerner died in 1991 of kidney failure at the age of eighty. Anne Schwerner, a retired high school biology teacher, was eighty-four years old when she died of Alzheimer's disease in 1996. Rita went on to law school, where she met and married a fellow law student. They moved to Seattle, Washington, where she worked as an attorney, had children, and eventually became a grandmother.

As the years passed, some in Neshoba County clinged to racist views, but violent resistance to racial change faded. The county's black citizens were able to exercise their right to vote and participated in civic affairs in the county. Desegregation of the county's public schools came about with relatively little friction. The Klan organization in Neshoba County declined significantly after the FBI's Mississippi Burning investigation. One federal government report in March 1971 indicated that the most recent meeting of the Klan in Neshoba County was comprised of only three men, two of whom were secretly agents for the bureau.

Attitudes and relationships can be complicated in a small town. Fenton DeWeese, a white attorney with historic family ties in Neshoba County, was known in the community as an advocate for the state of Mississippi who could bring the suspects in the Mississippi Burning case to trial for murder. DeWeese had even made it known that he would help the state prosecute the case. On his daughter's first day of kindergarten in Philadelphia, Mississippi, she got on the wrong bus. She was mistakenly let off at a local day-care center. Cecil Price, no longer a law enforcement officer, was listening to the local police scan radio announcement regarding the missing child, and he went out looking for DeWeese's daughter. His daughter was found safe, but Cecil Price's attempt to help "opened my eyes to a different part of him," DeWeese recalled. Nevertheless, "it didn't change my mind about the fact how he didn't pay for the crime."

While public interest in the case seemed to diminish, it did not die. The story of the Neshoba County triple murder resurfaced in the years following Freedom Summer. In 1975, a two-part television docudrama about the case was aired nationally. In

Florence Mars holding her book, *Witness in Philadelphia*.

1977, the Louisiana State University Press published *Witness in Philadelphia* by Florence Mars, who described in detail the social history of Neshoba County, and how her closed community dealt with the murders and what was perceived as a challenge to the social structure.

The Chaney, Goodman, Schwerner case even surfaced in presidential politics. The annual Neshoba County Fair, known as Mississippi's Giant Houseparty, has been a major event in the state since 1889. In addition to entertainment, agricultural displays, horse racing, a beauty pageant, and other activities, the fair is an important forum for local, state, and sometimes national politicians. After Ronald Reagan received the Republican nomination for president in 1980, one of his first speeches in the general election campaign against incumbent President Jimmy Carter was delivered on August 3, 1980, at the Neshoba County Fair. At the fair, Mr. Reagan told a cheering and mostly white audience, "I believe in states' rights" and he pledged that as president he would do all he could to "restore to states and local governments the power that properly belongs to them." Some thought that Reagan's endorsement of states' rights was a coded appeal to southern racists and was considered particularly insensitive and offensive as the fairgrounds are located only a few miles from where the three civil rights workers were murdered. Mickey's brother, Steve Schwerner, observed that Reagan was "telling the South it's okay to be racist and that's what states' rights means. I can't imagine that he didn't know that, or at least his handlers must have known it."

After the 1967 federal trial, little happened to move the state of Mississippi forward to reopen the case and initiate a prosecution for murder. But this began to change in 1989 as a result of the efforts of a number of Mississippians.

Stanley Dearman moved to Neshoba County as a young man and brought a unique perspective to the case. He covered the case as a reporter for the *Meridian Star*, and he would play a role in bringing the case to justice when he moved to Philadelphia. Dearman was born and raised in Meridian. When he covered the Meridian Police Department during his time as a reporter at the *Meridian Star*, he had an opportunity to observe how the police treated black people. In the early 1960s, he observed that the Meridian Police Department was "wall-to-wall Klan." Dearman saw a black man brought into the police station. When the black man responded to a question from the police sergeant, the sergeant reached over the counter and punched him in the face and said, "You say 'sir' to me!" Dearman often observed similar incidents of physical abuse against black people.

After his stint at the *Meridian Star*, he went to Philadelphia in late 1966 to run the *Neshoba Democrat*, the weekly newspaper of Neshoba County, and bought the paper in 1968. Early on, the *Neshoba Democrat*, like many southern newspapers at the time, didn't publish news about the black community, such as not carrying wedding announcements for black people. This treatment of the black community "had become second nature to most people," he recalled. For years after the 1967 federal trial, it was generally assumed that there would be no effort by Mississippi to try the Mississippi Burning suspects for murder. Stanley Dearman referred to these as the "years of futility." It was clear that "nobody was going to take any initiative to bring this case to trial."

The Mount Zion Methodist Church in Longdale commemorates the Chaney, Goodman, Schwerner murders every year. The 1989 memorial service, commemorating the twenty-fifth anniversary of the murders, was particularly meaningful. A group of local citizens worked to provide support for the commemoration. Stanley Dearman recalled that "the major industries around town each contributed $10,000 for food and logistical support." He thought "it was amazing that the community started coming together to put on this memorial service." The 1989 memorial was the first visit to Neshoba County for several family members of the victims, and Dearman thought it would be important for the community to know the victims better.

In April 1989, Dearman won a fund-raising raffle to travel to New York City and attend the Metropolitan Opera. He decided to combine his brief stay in New York with an interview of Carolyn Goodman. The two hit it off immediately. In the interview, she talked at length about who Andy was as a person. To the readers of the *Neshoba Democrat*, Dearman's interview with Carolyn put a human face on Andrew Goodman, and Andy became more than simply a photograph on the FBI's famous MISSING poster. The interview had a "profound effect" on the local community. Readers told Dearman, "I'm so glad you did that. We never thought of it like that before."

Carolyn Goodman and other members of the victims' families came to Neshoba County for the twenty-fifth anniversary commemoration. Mickey's brother, Steve Schwerner, found the twenty-fifth anniversary commemoration to be a "very moving" experience. He recalled that "[i]t was especially nice seeing people coming up to Rita and saying how 'I was in the freedom school when I was a little girl and you changed my life.' That was very touching." Andy's friend Ralph Engelman said at the event, "I think it's important for younger people to remember that there was a time when

At a fortieth anniversary commemoration of the murder of the three civil rights workers at Mount Zion United Methodist Church on June 20, 2004, are *(foreground, left to right)* Stanley Dearman, Carolyn Goodman, and Dave Dennis, along with other civil rights veterans.

blacks and whites, Jews and gentiles struggled together and even died together."

The 1989 memorial would be significant for another reason. That year, Neshoba County native Dick Molpus was serving as secretary of state of Mississippi. With the twenty-fifth anniversary of the triple murders approaching, he realized that it was a significant event in the history of his hometown and his state. In twenty-five years, no Mississippi government official had expressed remorse at the murder of the three men, which had taken place with the involvement of law enforcement officials. He intended to change that. As a state official, Molpus felt a special obligation to address the triple murders publicly. "All of us have certain points in our life where kind of the stars align and you're either called to step forward, or either you step back, and I felt like it was just my time to step forward."

At the memorial service, Dick Molpus directed his comments particularly at the families of the three victims:

> We deeply regret what happened here twenty-five years ago. We wish we could undo it. We are profoundly sorry that they are gone. We wish we could bring them back. Every decent person in Philadelphia and Neshoba County and Mississippi feels that way. . . . My heart is full because I know that for a long time, many of us have been searching for a way to ease the burden that this community has carried for twenty-five years, but we have never known quite

what to do or say. But today we know one way. Today we pay tribute to those who died. We acknowledge that dark corner of our past. . . . So to you, the families, I say: Listen to the words that will be said today. But most of all, see what is around you. Draw strength and solace from it. Know that it is real. Black, white, and Choctaw Indian together have forged a new and strong bond and helped transform a community. Fear has waned — fear of the unknown, fear of each other — and hope abides. That is our story. And you and yours are part of it. God bless each of you. We are genuinely glad to have you here.

Family members of the murdered men were touched by the apology, as were many in the local community. "It was a brave thing for him to do," noted Stanley Dearman, and it "started a trend in the community of people coming around" on the issue. Molpus recalled: "I got an enormous response from people who had a conscience, who I care about." The twenty-fifth anniversary built up momentum for reexamining the case for prosecution. However, the apology also got Molpus a number of death threats, which required him to have security for several months after the speech. When Molpus ran for governor of Mississippi in 1995, his apology was a significant issue in the campaign.

The release of the film *Mississippi Burning* brought new awareness to the case. Perhaps the most important fan of the film would turn out to be a young reporter for the Jackson, Mississippi, *Clarion-Ledger* named Jerry Mitchell. Alan Parker's film, starring Gene Hackman and Willem Dafoe, based on the Chaney, Goodman, Schwerner case, was publicly released in late 1988. Some were critical of the film, in part because of the portrayal of FBI agents as heroes when J. Edgar Hoover was hostile to the civil rights movement, and because the blacks in the film were considered to be portrayed as being generally passive when so many blacks took enormous risks in their fight for equality. Nevertheless, many found the film compelling, graphically depicting the racism and violence of the time. Mitchell attended a screening of the film in January 1989 with two FBI agents who worked on the case. He found it to be a "very powerful film" and not a film "you could sit and watch and be neutral about." When the film was over, Mitchell asked the agents questions about what really happened in the case. This began the reporter's education in the civil rights movement.

After seeing the film, Mitchell started writing about the status of the case. In 1990, another film dramatizing the case, *Murder in Mississippi*, was televised nationally, keeping the story alive in the nation's conscience. Mitchell delved into the case and wrote stories for the *Clarion-Ledger* — "the more I wrote about it, the more I got feedback on it." Mitchell and his editors would receive complaints such as, "What are you doing digging up the past? Why don't you write about something that's going on now?" This kind of response would increase over the years as Mitchell continued to write about this and other civil rights cases, but he was relentless and fearless.

Shortly after *Mississippi Burning* was released, Mitchell learned that Mississippi attorney general Mike Moore was quietly examining the case to determine whether it could be successfully prosecuted. However, throughout the 1990s, Moore declined to move forward with any prosecutions in the case. A development related to Sam Bowers, the Imperial Wizard of the White Knights of the Ku Klux Klan, would give added impetus to reopen the case. In addition to his conviction in the Mississippi Burning case, in 1998, Bowers would finally be convicted and sentenced to life in prison for his role in the firebombing of the home of civil rights activist Vernon Dahmer Sr. near Hattiesburg, Mississippi. Dahmer was killed in the attack, and Sam Bowers was brought to trial five times for his role in Dahmer's murder.

In January 1984, Bowers had given an oral-history interview with the Mississippi Department of Archives and History, in which he stated of his conviction in the Mississippi Burning case that "I was quite delighted to be convicted and have the main instigator of the entire affair walk out of the courtroom a free man, which everybody — including the trial judge and the prosecutors and everybody else knows that that happened." Jerry Mitchell uncovered and reported on this interview, which was not to be publicly released until after Bowers's death. While he did not cite him by name, it was apparent that the "main instigator" Bowers was referring to was Edgar Ray Killen. The revelation prompted several of the victims' family members, including Rita Schwerner Bender, Ben Chaney, and Carolyn Goodman, to call for the Mississippi attorney general to reopen the case.

Gradually, Mississippi was coming to terms with its segregationist past. For example, the Mississippi State Sovereignty Commission was shut down in 1977, and its files were opened to the public in March 1998. Among many things, the files showed how the state spy agency had monitored the activities of the Schwerners and other civil rights activists and passed this information along to local law enforcement officials.

Early in 1999, Mississippi attorney general Michael Moore reopened the case, with the Justice Department providing the attorney general's office with some forty thousand pages of FBI files related to the case. One promising aspect of the state's efforts to bring indictments against the individuals involved in the triple murder were conversations between Cecil Price and officials in the attorney general's office, which began in 2000. They held out the hope that Price would at last be willing to discuss his involvement in the murders and to implicate others. However, those hopes were dashed the following year.

In May 2001, Cecil Price died at the University of Mississippi Medical Center in Jackson, the same facility where he observed the autopsies of the three young men in August 1964. He died of a skull fracture after he took a fall from a cherry picker. Mike Moore saw Price's death as a serious setback to any potential effort by the state to prosecute the case: "If he had been a defendant, he would have been a principal defendant. If he had been a witness, he would have been our best witness. Either way, his death is a tragic blow to our case." With this and other setbacks, by the end of 2002, it appeared that the state of Mississippi was unlikely to bring murder charges in the case.

During this period, members of the Neshoba community also came together to press the state for a new trial. In 2000, Stanley Dearman wrote an editorial in the *Neshoba Democrat* calling for an accounting in the case. "This is a case that never goes away for the reason that it has never been dealt with in the way it should have been. It's time to bring a conclusion by applying the rule of law. Come hell or high water, it's time for an accounting." Dearman would continue to call for the state to open up the case for prosecution.

In 2004, Dick Molpus, now retired from public office and a prominent Mississippi businessman, was invited to attend a meeting of Neshoba County community leaders. At the conclusion of his remarks, he was asked his opinion on how Neshoba County's economy could be improved. Molpus responded by addressing the "big elephant" in the room. He said that as a practical matter, "no one of any reputation is going to come here unless we address the fact that these murderers are still running loose." This failure said something about the county's moral fiber and whether there was a commitment to justice. Many in the audience agreed with this assessment, and Molpus suggested that Dr. Susan Glisson, executive director of Mississippi's William Winter Institute for Racial Reconciliation, work with people in Neshoba County to put together a coalition of interested and concerned citizens. And what became the Philadelphia Coalition took off.

In short order, the Philadelphia Coalition was formed, and it was comprised of approximately thirty citizens of Neshoba County, including black and white community leaders, members of the local Choctaw Indian tribe, elected officials, and people in business. The coalition's cochairs were Jim Prince, who had taken over the ownership of the *Neshoba Democrat* from Stanley Dearman, and Leroy Clemons, head of the local chapter of the NAACP. While racial reconciliation was an important part of the coalition's efforts, it was ultimately decided that there couldn't be reconciliation until there was justice in the Mississippi Burning case.

The fortieth anniversary of the murders was to be commemorated in June 2004, which was also the fiftieth anniversary of the famous *Brown v. Board of Education* Supreme Court ruling, and members of the Philadelphia Coalition realized there would be a great deal of press attention regarding the Mississippi Burning case. In May 2004, the Philadelphia Coalition held a press conference to release its call for justice in the case. Their statement said, in part, that "[w]ith firm resolve and strong belief in the rule of law, we call on the Neshoba County District Attorney, the state Attorney General and the US Department of Justice to make every effort to seek justice in this case. We deplore the possibility that history will record that the state of Mississippi, and this community in particular, did not make a good faith effort to do its duty." In Jerry Mitchell's view, the successful effort to bring Edgar Ray Killen to justice for his role in the murders of the three civil rights workers "wouldn't have happened without the coalition," a view shared by Dick Molpus. Other Neshoba County officials expressed support for the coalition and its objectives.

The year 2004 would also see a new district attorney for Neshoba County, Mark Duncan, as well as a new attorney general for the state of Mississippi, Jim Hood. Both men became committed to bringing the case to a grand jury if they felt they were able to obtain sufficient evidence that could lead to a conviction. The two men and their staffs con-ducted an in-depth review of the case. On September 14, 2004, Attorney General Jim Hood met with the Philadelphia Coalition at their invitation. Carolyn Goodman and her son David also attended the meeting. Carolyn talked about Andy, humanizing him to the meeting attendees. David Goodman told Hood, "Sometimes you try a case

Dick Molpus addresses the fortieth anniversary commemoration.

even if you think you're going to lose because it's important. This country, Mississippi, and Neshoba County want to see something done." It was an emotional session. Hood would not discuss the specifics of the investigation, but he noted that he and Mark Duncan were coming close to a decision about whether to take the evidence they had to the Neshoba County grand jury.

Prosecutors laid out before the grand jury the available evidence against all eight of the surviving defendants in the 1967 trial. The grand jury concluded that there was sufficient evidence to indict only one individual. For the public, the suspense soon ended. On January 6, 2005, a Neshoba County grand jury indicted Edgar Ray Killen for his role in the murders of James Chaney, Andrew Goodman, and Michael Schwerner. As Attorney General Jim Hood stated, "We presented everyone who was living . . . for potential indictment, and they came and indicted Edgar Ray Killen."

CHAPTER 9
THE TRIAL OF EDGAR RAY KILLEN

*Who the hell [does] he think he is to take somebody's life?
Who died and made him God? And I would like him to tell
me what made him think he can kill somebody and get
away with it?*

— Barbara Chaney-Dailey, sister of James Chaney, on
Edgar Ray Killen

Several years before Edgar Ray Killen was indicted by the state
of Mississippi, reporter Jeffrey Goldberg went to Killen's house
southeast of Philadelphia, Mississippi. Preacher Killen's home
was a short distance from the location where the three men
were murdered on Rock Cut Road. Holding a shotgun, Killen
told the reporter, "I told you I ain't talking with you. My
gun's clean and ready." The reporter observed that Killen
was "leathery and bent over, but his arms were roped with
muscle. He seemed to be living proof that time does not tem-
per rage. He was seventy-six when I saw him. 'I told you I
don't want to talk about those boys no more,'" Killen said.
Goldberg told Killen about a conversation the reporter had
with Stanley Dearman, who at the time was still editor of the
Neshoba Democrat. Dearman had told Goldberg that several

people were thinking of building a memorial to the three young men, which "sent Killen into a rage." "A memorial?" Killen asked. "To who? The dead guys?" Goldberg nodded in the affirmative. "Never!" Killen shouted. "It'll never happen." Killen then told the reporter, "I'm not a man of violence, but if you don't get off my property right now, I'm going to shoot you dead." Goldberg got into his car. "The dogs gave chase, and I tried hard not to run them over. Killen came out to the road. In my rearview mirror, I saw his face, contorted in fury, slowly disappear."

Killen's role as a Klansman and his role in the murders were extensively covered in the 1967 federal trial. James Jordan had given testimony that on June 21, 1964, Preacher Killen had recruited Klansmen to participate in the murders and directed what was to be done that night. Killen made sure he would not be present when the murders were committed, and his alibi would be attending a wake at a funeral home in Philadelphia. According to Jordan's testimony at the 1967 trial, Killen told his fellow Klansmen that "if anything happened, I'd be the first one they'd question." Yet despite the strength of the testimony against Killen at the 1967 trial, the jury was unable to reach a verdict. A mistrial was declared for him, and Killen went free. Jerry Mitchell later discovered that eleven of the twelve jurors were willing to convict Killen, but one lone juror held out. She could never vote guilty against Killen: "For one reason — she could never convict a preacher."

But many believed that Edgar Ray Killen played a key role in the murders. As Stanley Dearman observed, "Edgar

Ray Killen was the ringleader. He was the producer and director." "I talked to him a lot of times," said Dearman, "but he was reluctant to talk about the case. He would talk about everything except the case." After the 1967 trial, Killen returned to his life in Neshoba County as the owner-operator of a sawmill and a part-time Baptist preacher. He claimed to remain popular in the community: "I don't really think among my neighbors and the people that come testify for me, I don't have to prove anything. I'm not meaning this as a brag or anything, but I'm literally mobbed most anywhere I go by people that know me. And I appreciate it."

Edgar Ray Killen had another run-in with the law in 1975, when he was brought to trial and convicted of making a telephone call threatening someone's life. Killen refused a plea agreement, which would have required him to apologize to the offended family and promise to not bother them again.

Jerry Mitchell, investigative reporter for the Clarion-Ledger newspaper

So he served five months in Mississippi State Penitentiary at Parchman for the offense. The district attorney prosecuting this case was Marcus Gordon, who later became a circuit judge and would be the presiding judge over Killen's 2005 trial in the Mississippi Burning case.

Jerry Mitchell had talked to Edgar Ray Killen several times on the telephone and was ultimately able to persuade Killen to meet with him in person. Mitchell took Killen and his wife to a restaurant to eat catfish, a popular meal in Mississippi. "It was interesting," Mitchell recalled of the meeting. Killen denied any involvement in the murder of the three civil rights workers. Nevertheless, Mitchell asked him, "Well, what do you think should happen to the people who were involved?" Killen responded, "Well, I'm not going to say they were wrong."

Killen then proceeded to tell Mitchell a story regarding Martin Luther King Jr.'s assassination on April 4, 1968. Immediately after King's murder, the FBI deployed agents around the country to interview a number of white suprema-cists in an effort to find the assassin. Two agents interviewed Killen and asked him about his whereabouts on the day of the assassination. Killen refused to tell the agents anything. One of the agents left his card with Killen. After some time passed, Killen telephoned the FBI and asked to know who killed King. The FBI agent asked why he wanted to know. Killen replied that he "wanted to shake his hand."

The beginning of Edgar Ray Killen's trial was delayed because a tree fell on him in March 2005, breaking his bones in both thighs. Because Killen needed time to recuperate, Judge Marcus Gordon set the trial to start on June 13, 2005, at the Neshoba County Courthouse in Philadelphia, Mississippi. When the court convened on June 13, the first several days were spent on the jury selection process. From the small community's jury pool, a number of individuals were dismissed from serving for reasons as varied as health, financial hardship, fear for their safety, sympathy to Killen because of his age and/or health problems, unshakable opinions about the case, or because they were friends or relatives — however distant — of the defendant. Seventeen citizens were impaneled (twelve jury members and five alternates), and the group was comprised of four white men, nine white women, two black men, and two black women. Press attention to the trial was enormous, with news media converging on the Neshoba County Courthouse from throughout the state, the nation, and the world.

Under heavy guard, defendant Edgar Ray Killen is escorted into the Neshoba County Courthouse in Philadelphia, Mississippi, during his 2005 trial.

The state's prosecution was conducted by Attorney General Jim Hood and Neshoba County district attorney Mark Duncan. The prosecution's case against Edgar Ray Killen was challenging. At the time of the 2005 trial, seven of the original defendants from the 1967 trial, in addition to Edgar Ray Killen, were still alive. None of them would testify before the grand jury in exchange for immunity from prosecution. However, under state guidelines, previous confessions and other statements related to the crime were admissible in the Killen trial if the witness was cross-examined in the previous court proceeding in 1967.

The prosecution made more than half of its case against the defendant by relying on individuals reading testimony from the earlier trial in which several Klansmen identified Killen as the mastermind behind the murders. In addition to the Klansmen, the Neshoba County jurors heard from other dead witnesses from the jury trial almost thirty-eight years before, such as a highway patrolman and the Philadelphia jailer's wife.

Joseph "Mike" Hatcher, a former Klansman, had been a witness at the 1967 trial and was a prosecution witness in 2005. Unlike many other Klan witnesses from the

Jim Hood (left) and Mark Duncan review prosecution strategy.

1960s, he had not been paid by the FBI. Hatcher, who was a Meridian policeman in 1964, testified that the day after the murders, Killen told him that the three had been buried in an earthen dam "off Highway 21 where a pond was being built." However, when cross-examined, Hatcher conceded that he did not have personal knowledge of any evidence that showed that Killen committed the murders, and Killen had not claimed to organize the murder of the three men.

Among the other prosecution witnesses were family members of the victims. Rita Schwerner Bender took the stand and recounted the work that she and Mickey had undertaken to help Mississippi blacks and the relentless harassment the Schwerners received for doing so. After her testimony, she told reporters on the courthouse lawn: "You're treating this trial as the most important trial of the civil rights movement because two of these three men were white. That means we all have a discussion about racism in this country that has to continue. And if this trial is a way for you to all acknowledge that, for us to all acknowledge that and to have that discussion openly, then this trial has meaning."

During a recess, Rita Schwerner Bender *(left)* greets Barbara Chaney-Dailey and Ben Chaney.

Carolyn Goodman, eighty-nine years old, took the stand to talk about Andy and his desire to go to Mississippi. The experience was stressful for her. Indeed, the drive to Philadelphia for the trial had been emotionally difficult. "I'd driven on all that red Mississippi dirt, and somehow or other I envisioned Andy and those kids driving up there. . . . I have a pretty good imagination, and it just flooded me with feelings. This setting, seeing it as he had seen it, and driving up that same route that he drove, that just sort of got to me." She left Mississippi before the trial concluded.

Eighty-two-year-old Fannie Lee Chaney was the final prosecution witness. While she was ill and walked with a cane to the witness stand, she was determined to speak out for her son. As her daughter Julia noted, "She lived for that moment." Nevertheless, while her brief testimony and that of the other family members was emotional, none of them could provide testimony connecting Edgar Ray Killen to the murder of their loved ones.

The defense had a number of their own witnesses, including several who testified in support of Edgar Ray Killen's alibi that he was elsewhere when the murders occurred, as well as others who testified in support of his character. The defense conceded to the jury that Edgar Ray Killen was a member of the Ku Klux Klan, and a Kleagle, or recruiter — an affiliation Killen had long denied — and even recruited people to beat up the three young men but not to kill them. The prosecution, however, argued that the defendant did far

Dr. Carolyn Goodman, escorted by her son David, leaves the
Neshoba County Courthouse during the Killen trial.

Fannie Lee Chaney takes the stand at Edgar Ray Killen's trial
as the final prosecution witness.

more than recruit fellow Klansmen to inflict a beating. They argued that Killen, though not present at the shooting and burial, was the mastermind behind the murders.

As the case headed toward a verdict, each side made its closing argument. "Is a Neshoba County jury going to tell the rest of the world that we are not going to let Edgar Ray Killen get away with murder anymore? Not one day more! For forty-one years tomorrow, it's been Edgar Ray Killen and his friends who have written the history of Neshoba County," said Mark Duncan. In Attorney General Jim Hood's closing argument, he said of Killen, "He wants you to be weak and not do your duty to find him guilty of this crime. This is the man right here that has that venom, and there he sits, wanting your sympathy. What he doesn't want you to know is that he left these young boys in a grave, no funeral, no casket, dumped in there like a dog." Pointing his finger at Killen, sitting a short distance away, Hood added that "Killen is a coward."

On June 21, 2005, forty-one years to the day since James Chaney, Andrew Goodman, and Michael Schwerner were murdered in Neshoba County, the jury returned from its deliberations with a unanimous verdict for Edgar Ray Killen for three counts of manslaughter. Under Mississippi law, juries in murder trials are allowed to consider a lesser charge of manslaughter if requested by the prosecution. Because of the lack of new information related to the case, the prosecution had requested that the lesser charge of manslaughter become part of the Killen jury's consideration. Judge Gordon

Edgar Ray Killen *(right)* pleads not guilty to murder charges related to the three civil rights workers before Judge Marcus Gordon at the Neshoba County Courthouse in Philadelphia, Mississippi, on January 7, 2005.

granted this request. Murder means to kill someone with intent and malice aforethought, while manslaughter means to kill without a prior intention to kill.

After the verdict was announced, Rita Schwerner Bender expressed her disappointment that Killen was found guilty of manslaughter rather than murder. She said, "The fact that some members of this jury could have sat through that testimony, indeed could have lived here all these years and could not bring themselves to acknowledge that these were murders, that they were committed with malice, indicates that there are still people unfortunately among you who choose to look aside, who choose to not see the truth." But this appeared to be a minority view. Jewel Rush was relieved that the jury had been given the option of finding Killen guilty of manslaughter. She later commented, "[I]f he had gone for murder they would have found him not guilty." The prosecution stated they were not disappointed with the manslaughter verdict. Neshoba County district attorney Mark Duncan stated, "We were asking a lot to have the jury convict someone of murder when three of our four main witnesses were dead. The jury held Edgar Ray Killen accountable."

Two days after the jury returned its verdict, Judge Gordon sentenced Edgar Ray Killen to the maximum sentence of twenty years in prison for each of the three counts — a total of sixty years. Whether he was convicted of murder or manslaughter, the practical effect was the same: eighty-year-old Edgar Ray Killen had been held accountable by a unanimous jury of Neshoba County citizens —
both black and white — for his role in the deaths of James Chaney, Andrew Goodman, and Michael Schwerner, and was going to spend the rest of his life in jail for those crimes.

The verdict had special meaning to the families of the victims. Ben Chaney

Jewel Rush McDonald

At the 2005 Killen murder trial are *(front, left)* Rita Schwerner Bender and Dr. Carolyn Goodman; *(rear, left to right)* Mississippi attorney general Jim Hood, Neshoba County district attorney Mark Duncan, and David Goodman.

characterized his eighty-two-year-old mother as being happy about the verdict. "She finally believes that the life of her son has some value to the people in this community." Fannie Lee Chaney died in February 2007 at the age of eighty-four. She was buried next to her oldest son in a churchyard outside of Meridian, Mississippi. Later, in August of that year, Carolyn Goodman died at her home on New York's Upper West Side, after a series of strokes and seizures. She was ninety-one years old and was buried next to Andy and her husband, Robert. Both Fannie Lee and Carolyn lived to see a measure of justice for their sons.

AFTERWORD
TOWARD THE BELOVED COMMUNITY

*I just hoped this case would go away and leave me alone.
But it didn't. And I don't think from the time this case
happened, to this very day, that there hasn't been a single
day in all these years that I haven't thought about this case
and dwelled on it. And some little fleeting thought would
cause me to remember this case. It just gets in your system
and it holds. Yeah, this was a growing experience with me.
I mean, I didn't enter into all this with these same feelings
that I have now. But you get to think. . . . And there is no
other way to look at it and deal with it without trying to do
the right thing. You just can't dismiss it.*

— Stanley Dearman, former editor of the *Neshoba
Democrat*

Dr. Martin Luther King Jr.'s commitment to nonviolence in
the pursuit of social justice was rooted in his conception of
what he termed "the Beloved Community," which was attain-
able when enough people in the world became committed to
the methods and philosophy of nonviolence. He believed that
it was essential to break the cycle of retaliation and revenge
by not hating one's enemies. As he said in a speech in 1956,

"The end is reconciliation; the end is redemption; the end is the creation of the Beloved Community. It is this type of spirit and this type of love that can transform opponents into friends." Dr. King dreamed of a fully integrated society where unity would be an essential part of every aspect of social life. James, Andy, and Mickey, like Dr. King, fought and died for this nonviolent ideal.

Countless people took tremendous risks in the fight for civil rights and many of them lost their lives. Yet the Chaney, Goodman, Schwerner case was one of the most famous events of the civil rights era and received tremendous press attention. "It woke up America," says Andy's brother David Goodman of the murders. The memory of the three men and their sacrifice remains alive in the nation's consciousness, even decades after their murders.

When he was running for president in 2008, Barack Obama gave a speech before a prominent Jewish organization where he invoked the memory of the three civil rights workers: "In the great social movements in our country's history, Jewish- and African-Americans have stood shoulder to shoulder. They took buses down south together. They marched together. They bled together. And Jewish-Americans, like Andrew Goodman and Michael Schwerner, were willing to die alongside a black man, James Chaney, on behalf of freedom and on behalf of equality. Their legacy is our inheritance."

Ultimately, the three men were not simply murdered by members of the Ku Klux Klan. In a sense, they were killed by institutional racism that in 1964 permeated every aspect of Mississippi's legal, political, and social order. The establishment and perpetuation of a system of racial segregation created a climate of hatred and fear where acts of violence were inevitable. Complicity in the murders of James Chaney, Andrew Goodman, and Michael Schwerner extended far beyond the circle of racist thugs who gathered on Neshoba County's Rock Cut Road late on a summer's night.

The murder of the three civil rights workers had even more tangible meaning to the cause of civil rights. The efforts to outlaw discriminatory voting practices against black Americans gained considerable impetus from the national revulsion to the brutal murders of James Chaney, Andrew Goodman, and Michael Schwerner. The violent, unprovoked attack by Alabama state troopers on peaceful civil rights marchers crossing the Edmund Pettus Bridge in Selma, Alabama, in March 1965, finally persuaded the president and Congress to push for legislation, which became the Voting Rights Act of 1965. It was enacted into law on August 6, 1965. "J.E., Mickey, and Andy did not die in vain," stated Julia Chaney. "They have made an indelible imprint on this world." For Dick Molpus, the murder of the three men was "the defining moment in Mississippi."

The enfranchisement of blacks in Neshoba County, Mississippi, and throughout the South as a result of the Voting Rights Act of 1965, had a tremendous impact on the lives of black Americans. They were able to demand their rights and be heard through the ballot box. Paved streets, electricity, and mail service came to many southern black neighborhoods for the first time. Integration of schools and other public accommodations accelerated. Now, state and local officials who ignored the needs of their black constituents risked losing their jobs at the next election. And blacks ran for, and won, public office. A milestone was reached in May 2009 when James Young was elected the first black mayor of Philadelphia, a majority white town of 7,300 people. Neshoba County had come a long way since Freedom Summer. Eventually, Mississippi would come to

ANDREW GOODMAN
NOV.   23,   1943
JUNE   21,   1964

JAMES EARL CHANEY
MAY   30,   1943
JUNE   21,   1964

MICHAEL H. SCHWERNER
NOV.   6,   1939
JUNE   21,   1964

The memorial for Andrew Goodman, James Chaney, and Michael Schwerner at the Mount Nebo Missionary Baptist Church in Philadelphia, Mississippi. The memorial was dedicated on December 12, 1976.

have the largest number of black elected officials in the United States.

Many people feel that this country is not yet at the place where the killing of a black mother's son is as important as the killing of a white mother's son. But the United States is closer to that goal than it was in 1964.

James Chaney, Andrew Goodman, and Michael Schwerner lived relatively short lives, but they were lives of consequence. They risked, and ultimately lost, their lives to make the world a better place by fighting against injustice, fear, ignorance, intolerance, hatred, and inequality. Those who believe in the importance of fighting against these things — like James, Andy, Mickey, and countless others — still cannot rest. Because, in the words of the song from that long-ago summer, freedom is a constant struggle.

SAINT: FANNIE LOU HAMER

Born in 1917, Fannie Lou Townsend was the youngest of twenty children. Her family lived in desperate poverty as sharecroppers on a plantation in the Mississippi Delta. "Life was worse than hard," she recalled of her youth. "It was *horrible*! We never did have enough to eat, and I don't remember how old I was when I got my first pair of shoes, but I was a big girl. Mama tried to keep our feet warm by wrapping them in rags and tying them with string." Her mother instilled in her and her siblings pride in themselves and their race. Hamer remembered, "Sometimes when things were so bad and I'd start thinking maybe it would be better if we were white, she'd insist we should be proud of being black, telling us, 'Nobody will respect you unless you stand up for yourself.'"

At the age of six, Fannie Lou began the backbreaking work of picking cotton. Though she was highly intelligent, because she needed to help her family, she never got past the sixth grade. She became Fannie Lou Hamer when she married Perry Hamer in 1944. They lived and worked on a plantation outside Ruleville, Mississippi. Unable to have her own children, Fannie Lou and her husband adopted two daughters and raised a number of other children as well.

A major turning point in Hamer's life occurred in August 1962 when she attended a mass meeting to discuss voting. At the meeting, Hamer heard a number of civil rights activists, including James Bevel, Bob Moses, James Forman, and Amzie Moore speak about the importance of voter registration. At the end of the meeting, one of the speakers asked the group, "Who will go on Friday to register?" Fannie Lou Hamer raised her hand, and she tried to register to vote. Word of her defiance of the racial status quo quickly made it back to Ruleville. The plantation owner angrily confronted Fannie Lou when she returned from the courthouse. "We are not ready for this in Mississippi." She replied, "I didn't register for you, I tried to register for myself." She was thrown off the plantation after working there for eighteen years. While the loss of her home and job pushed the Hamers into desperate poverty, it freed Fannie Lou to become involved in the civil rights movement. There was nothing more that Mississippi's white society could take away from her.

During her years as a civil rights advocate, Hamer was arrested, shot at, and beaten. But her deep religious faith kept her from feeling hatred toward white people. Hamer was also passionately committed to America's ideals. Her courage and commitment to justice inspired many.

When civil rights leaders were planning Freedom Summer, she was a strong advocate for the inclusion of white student volunteers. "If we're trying to break down this barrier of segregation, we can't segregate ourselves," she argued. She later went to Oxford, Ohio, to train the summer volunteers. She taught the young people what to expect in Mississippi and what they should know about the people with whom they'd be working.

Shortly before she died, Hamer talked about her belief that people could do anything:

A living example was Andy Goodman, James Chaney, and Michael Schwerner that come down here. And I remember talking to them the Sunday before they went to Oxford, Ohio, for the orientation where we had to drill or talk to them about what they might be faced with. Even when Christ hung on the cross, he said greater love has no man than the one who is willing to lay down his life for his friends. Even though they was aware they might die, they still came. These are the things we have to think about. These are the things we can't sweep under the rug. And these are the things that still give me hope.

VISIONARY: BOB MOSES

An angry white police officer got out of his police car and came up to the young black man. It was August 1961 in McComb, Mississippi. The police officer asked the young man, Bob Moses, whether he was the "nigger that came down from New York to stir up a lot of trouble?" The young man replied, "I'm the Negro who came down from New York to instruct people in voter registration." The officer did not react well when Moses took down his name. "Get in the car, nigger!" Taken back to the police station, the unflappable civil rights worker asked for his one phone call traditionally given to those arrested. Moses placed a collect phone call to the Justice Department in Washington, DC, where John Doar accepted the charges. Moses recounted the violation of civil rights law and suggested the possibility of a federal investigation. Southern authorities in this era of brutal segregation weren't used to dealing with black people like Bob Moses.

Robert Parris Moses was born in 1935 and grew up in New York City, where he attended Stuyvesant High School, a public school for gifted students. After attending Hamilton College in upstate New York, where he won a scholarship, Moses received a master of arts degree from Harvard in 1957 and entered the university's doctoral program in philosophy. However, when his mother died, he withdrew from Harvard and remained in New York City to look after his ailing father. Moses went on to teach mathematics to high school students at New York City's prestigious Horace Mann School.

Bob Moses was galvanized by images in the press of the student sit-ins sweeping the country in an effort to fight segregation. Seeing the determined student protesters was a revelation to the young teacher. "Before the Negro in the South had always looked on the defensive, cringing. This time they were taking the initiative," Moses said. "They were kids my age, and I knew this had something to do with my own life. It made me realize that for a long time I had been troubled by the problem of being a Negro and at the same time being an American. This was the answer."

In the summer of 1960, Moses traveled to Georgia to work with Martin Luther King Jr.'s SCLC on a voter registration project. Moses became close to Ella Baker, a major force in the newly formed SNCC, who pushed the organization to become democratic in its decision making. An essential part of SNCC's approach was to encourage self-initiative in the civil rights struggle and to empower as many grassroots activists as possible to assume leadership roles. A premium was placed on listening to the views of others. Bob Moses came to this approach toward leadership naturally.

Moses soon realized that gaining Mississippi's blacks their right to vote was the key to positive change in the state. He played a major role in the effort to empower Mississippi's blacks through the ballot box, an approach that would lead to Freedom Summer. Reserved, determined, and brilliant, Bob Moses led by example, never suggesting that anyone take a risk he had not already taken. He became an important figure in the civil rights movement who was respected and emulated by many.

"You didn't wonder how she felt; she let it be known immediately," said Gerald "Boots" Howell of his lifelong friend Florence Mars. "She worked for those who didn't have what she did." An only child who never married, Florence Latimer Mars was raised in a prosperous and prominent old family with deep roots in Neshoba County. As she grew up in this small segregated society, she came to realize the inequalities that blacks were forced to endure. "I thought Negroes were supposed to be happy. I soon realized they had every reason not to be." Over the years, Mars would accumulate many black friends in her community.

Mars left Neshoba County to attend college; worked in Atlanta, Georgia, during World War II; and spent a great deal of her time in the 1950s living in New Orleans, where she indulged in her love of jazz and demonstrated considerable skill as a photographer chronicling life in that city. She returned to Neshoba County in 1962, where she would live for the remainder of her life. Mars raised a herd of purebred Hereford cattle on her farm and ran the Neshoba County Stockyards, which she had purchased in 1957.

Appalled at the murders committed in her county, Mars became one of the few white people in town willing to talk to

FBI investigators. In the small town of Philadelphia, Mars's cooperation with the "outsiders" marked her. She testified before a grand jury looking into the murders. Almost immediately, the Ku Klux Klan initiated a boycott of the stockyards and ran her out of business. She was ostracized by many in the community and was even forced to stop teaching the adult Bible class at First Methodist Church in Philadelphia.

Harassment against Mars came to a head when, returning home one evening from the Neshoba County Fair in the summer of 1965, she and a friend were pulled over and arrested by Sheriff Lawrence Rainey on trumped-up charges. Mars was arrested for "drunken driving and resisting arrest," and the two women were taken overnight to the same jail in which Chaney, Goodman, and Schwerner were held just more than a year before. This was in violation of southern tradition at that time, which held that if a white woman was considered to be unable to drive a vehicle for whatever reason, a law enforcement officer would simply drive her home rather than put her in jail. Mars reflected on her situation: "I had been disdainful of Rainey and certain that I was immune to his travesties. Now he had thrown me and Mary Ann [Welsh] in jail, and we were powerless to do anything about it. I had challenged the Klan, and I had lost. They had said they would ruin me and they had succeeded. I cried in disgrace and defeat and told Mary Ann that I was through — to hell with the town, the Klan could have it for all I cared." But Mars never gave up on Philadelphia or Neshoba County. The arrest of Florence Mars was a turning point that outraged many in the community and caused public opinion to shift away from Sheriff Rainey.

An astute and critical observer of her community, Mars wrote about the Freedom Summer murders and the impact they had on Neshoba County. Part autobiography and part local history, Mars's book, *Witness in Philadelphia*, became a minor classic in civil rights literature. In its review of her 1977 work, the *New York Times* stated, "Her book makes compelling reading; it should be in every school in the country, to teach young people what the unmasked face of bigotry looks like and about the quiet, difficult courage of ordinary people like Florence Mars."

Florence Mars lived to see Edgar Ray Killen tried in her hometown's courthouse for the murder of the three men. Though confined to a wheelchair, Mars attended the trial every day and listened to everything that went on. Fenton DeWeese said of her, "She was our conscience, our guide along the path to resolution and redemption for our community."

INVESTIGATOR: JERRY MITCHELL

The makers of 1988's *Mississippi Burning* could not have imagined the role their film would play in launching one of the most distinguished journalistic careers in the history of the American civil rights movement. Watching this film would spark Jerry Mitchell's interest in the American civil rights movement and evolve into a commitment to bring the killers of James Chaney, Andrew Goodman, and Michael Schwerner — as well as other civil rights–era criminals — to justice.

Born in 1959, Jerry Mitchell grew up in Texas. He was distant from the racial strife affecting the nation during the 1960s, noting that it was "almost like it took place on another planet." When Jerry Mitchell was a boy, one of his friends used the word *nigger*, and Mitchell then used that word at home. "And my mom treated me like I committed a capital offense. And I'm very grateful for that." He loved music, particularly the Beatles and other artists from the 1960s. As Mitchell grew older, in addition to staying connected with the music of the era, he read more about the civil rights movement. After college, he became a reporter and went to work for Jackson, Mississippi's, *Clarion-Ledger* newspaper in 1986.

Mitchell's investigative work led to the reopening of the case for the assassination of civil rights leader Medgar Evers. The suspected assassin was Byron De La Beckwith, a Klansman and virulent racist who had been tried twice in 1964 before all-white male juries that were unable to reach verdicts in the case. Mitchell's investigative work led to Beckwith's conviction in 1994. When the guilty verdict was rendered, Mitchell recalled, "I felt chills going down my spine. It was the most amazing thing I ever witnessed." Several days after the trial ended, a sheriff informed Mitchell that as Beckwith was being led away from the courthouse, he kept muttering Jerry Mitchell's name over and over. The sheriff warned Mitchell, "If I were you, Jerry, I'd go home a different way each night."

Jerry Mitchell's reporting also played a key role in the successful conviction of Ku Klux Klan Imperial Wizard Sam Bowers for ordering the 1966 firebombing of the Hattiesburg, Mississippi, home of civil rights activist Vernon Dahmer. Bowers's first four trials for the Dahmer murder ended in hung juries, but in large part because of Mitchell's reporting, Bowers was finally convicted in 1998 and sentenced to life in prison. (Bowers had previously served six years in federal prison for his role in the 1964 killings of James Chaney, Andrew Goodman, and Michael Schwerner.) Mitchell's efforts also led to the 2002 trial and conviction of Bobby Frank Cherry, one of the last surviving suspects in the 1963 church bombing in Birmingham, Alabama, that resulted in the death of four girls.

Mitchell considered the Chaney, Goodman, Schwerner murders "by far the hardest case of the ones I've worked on, in terms of getting answers." Nevertheless, he was ultimately instrumental in bringing Edgar Ray Killen to justice for his role in the murders. Neshoba County native and former Mississippi secretary of state Dick Molpus is emphatic about Mitchell's role in the Mississippi Burning case. "Edgar Ray Killen would not have been brought to justice without Jerry Mitchell. Jerry invented the word *relentless*. . . . Jerry is a bona fide, living, breathing Mississippi hero."

MAP OF MISSISSIPPI

MISSISSIPPI

CITIES
- ⊛ State capitals
- ● County seats
- • Cities

BOUNDARIES
- —— State
- —— County

TENNESSEE

ARKANSAS

LOUISIANA

ALABAMA

Hernando • Holly Springs • Ashland • Corinth • Iuka
Tunica • Coldwater • Ripley • Booneville
Senatobia • Blue Mountain • New Albany
Sardis • Belmont

Marks • Batesville • Oxford • Pontotoc • Fulton
Clarksdale • Tupelo
Charleston • Water Valley • Okolona
Rosedale • Sumner • Coffeeville • Pittsboro • Aberdeen
Drew • Grenada • Houston
Cleveland • West Point
Greenwood • Carrollton • Eupora • Walthall • Columbus
Indianola • Winona • Starkville
Greenville • Vaiden • Ackerman • Brooksville
Belzoni
Hollandale • Lexington • Ethel • Louisville • Macon
Kosciusko • Shuqualak
Mayersville • Rolling Fork • Pickens • Noxapater • De Kalb
Yazoo City • Carthage • Philadelphia
Bentonia • Canton • Lauderdale
Madison • Sebastopol • Decatur • Meridian
Vicksburg • Jackson • Forest • Newton
Raymond • Pearl • Brandon • Hickory
Utica • Terry
Port Gibson • Crystal Springs • Raleigh • Paulding • Quitman
Alcorn • Mendenhall • Magee • Bay Springs
Fayette • Hazelhurst • Sandersville
Natchez • Meadville • Prentiss • Collins • Laurel • Waynesboro
Brookhaven • Monticello • Ellisville • Buckatunna
Crosby • Hattiesburg • State Line
Summit • Columbia • Pervis • New Augusta • Leakesville
Woodville • Liberty • Magnolia • Tylertown • Brooklyn
McComb
Poplarville • Wiggins • Lucedale

LOUISIANA

Picayune
Baton Rouge • Gulfport • Biloxi
Bay Saint Louis • Ocean Springs • Pascagoula

©1998, Encyclopædia Britannica, Inc.

ENDNOTES

PROLOGUE

"Be ashamed to die . . ." Mary Mann, *Life of Horace Mann* (Boston: Walker, Fuller, and Company, 1865) p. 575.

In June 1964, Willie Peacock . . . *We Are Not Afraid*, pp. 22–23

INTRODUCTION

"To be born black . . ." *Eyes on the Prize*, p. 222

Blacks in the South were second-class citizens at best . . . *Dark Journey*, p. 24

In its 1896 ruling in *Plessy v. Ferguson*, the US Supreme Court . . . *Mississippi: A History*, pp. 178, 277

The 1954 ruling in the case of *Brown v. Board of Education* . . . *Mississippi: A History*, p. 276

A July 1954 meeting of concerned whites in Indianola, Mississippi . . . *Local People*, p. 45

Its membership was comprised of white citizens . . . *Local People*, pp. 45–52

. . . the Mississippi State Sovereignty Commission was created on March 29, 1956. Sovereignty Commission Online; Agency History, Mississippi Department of Archives and History online at http://mdah.state.ms.us/arrec/digital_archives/sovcom /scagencycasehistory.php

. . . during the period from 1889 to 1945, more lynchings were held in Mississippi . . . *Dark Journey*, p. 229

Local authorities were seldom willing ... *Mississippi History Now*, an online publication of the Mississippi Historical Society; "Reconstruction in Mississippi, 1865–1876," by Jason Phillips, http://mshistory.k12.ms.us/index.php?id=204

On the evening of May 7, 1955, Reverend George W. Lee ... *Local People*, pp. 53–54

The victim was Lamar Smith ... *Local People*, p. 54

A significant milestone in the battle for equality ... *Eyes on the Prize*, pp. 213–18

In early June 1963, a group of civil rights activists ... *Local People*, p. 171

... a federal jury comprised of local white men in Oxford, Mississippi, found the accused not guilty. *Local People*, pp. 171–73

... just days after Fannie Lou Hamer's savage beating in Winona, Medgar Evers ... *Eyes on the Prize*, pp. 221–25

On Election Day, more than eighty-three thousand freedom votes were cast ... *Local People*, p. 205

Mississippi's civil rights leaders considered next steps, focusing on grassroots work ... *Local People*, p. 206

The Imperial Wizard, or leader, of the White Knights ... *Local People*, p. 217

By the middle of 1964, approximately five thousand white Mississippians had joined the Ku Klux Klan. *Local People*, p. 216

The volunteers were divided into two groups ... *Freedom Summer*, pp. 18–19

Doar was highly respected as a friend of the civil rights movement. *Freedom Summer*, p. 36

Jess Brown, one of only a handful of black lawyers in Mississippi ... *Freedom Summer*, p. 35

The murder of the three civil rights workers marked the height of armed resistance ... Stanley Dearman e-mail to author,

February 25, 2013: "This is a case that I've always thought of as being the high-water mark of armed resistance to change in the American South, particularly, Mississippi."

CHAPTER 1: A PLANNED DELIBERATE MURDER

"When historians weigh the sixth decade . . ." *Three Lives for Mississippi*, p. 6

"Lord, don't let them kill . . ." *New York Times*, June 28, 1964, "Mississippi Drags River in Search for Rights Aides," by Claude Sitton

. . . her prayer "struck the hearts of those men. . . ." *We Are Not Afraid*, p. 5

The white man told the other vigilantes, "Load up" . . . "Mississippi Drags River in Search for Rights Aides"

"At this point they asked us what kind of a meeting . . ." FBI signed statement of James Thomas Rush Jr., June 28, 1964; MIBURN files

"They pulled J.T. from the car and struck him . . ." FBI statement of Georgia Yvonne Rush, June 27, 1964; MIBURN files

"and she's all bloody and crying . . ." Jewel Rush McDonald interview, June 5, 2012, Choctaw, Mississippi

. . . "that somebody would shoot in the house . . ." Jewel Rush McDonald interview

"[i]f they're going to kill you, you might as well . . ." *New York Times Magazine*, December 27, 1964, "A Stranger in Philadelphia, Mississippi," by Joseph Lelyveld

"You have been slaves too long" . . . *We Are Not Afraid*, p. 2

On Friday evening, June 19 . . . For an overview of the Freedom Summer training program at Oxford, Ohio, see Julian Bond, "1964 Mississippi Freedom Summer," in *Freedom Is a Constant Struggle: An Anthology of the Mississippi Civil Rights Movement* pp. 78–83

"There was nothing very special about it." *We Are Not Afraid*, p. 34

... "all of us were delighted with him" ... *Three Lives for Mississippi*, p. 90

Impressed with his fellow New Yorker, Mickey invited Andy ... *We Are Not Afraid*, pp. 28–29

There were eight people in the station wagon ... *We Are Not Afraid*, p. 34

When they arrived in Meridian ... *We Are Not Afraid*, p. 35

Mickey and Andy had breakfast at a café ... *Three Lives for Mississippi*, p. 96

"They had to go back ..." *New York Times*, June 17, 2005, "Widow Recalls Ghosts of '64 at Rights Trial," by Shaila Dewan

... Roscoe Jones, a teenage civil rights worker ... Roscoe Jones interview, June 4, 2012, Meridian, Mississippi

"The Klan knew that the only way they could get him up there ..." Roscoe Jones interview

... "[o]urs wasn't a waiting operation. ..." *Three Lives for Mississippi*, pp. 96–97

"If you're not back at four, what time do I start calling?" *Three Lives for Mississippi*, p. 97

"Mickey was a kid; he was a loving fellow. ..." *New York Times*, June 20, 2005, "Rights Workers Honored as Trial in Their Killings Proceeds," by Shaila Dewan

When they came home, Jewel recalled ... Jewel Rush McDonald interview

... the three men took off for Meridian ... *We Are Not Afraid*, p. 18

... the community center staff began implementing emergency procedures. *We Are Not Afraid*, pp. 44–45

... Roscoe Jones believed that the worst had happened. Roscoe Jones interview

One of the witnesses was Klansman James Jordan. . . . FBI signed statement of James Edward Jordan, November 5, 1964; by Special Agent Roy Martin Mitchell and Special Agent John H. Proctor Jr.; MIBURN files, p. 2

Barnette stated that when he and other Klansmen arrived . . . FBI signed statement of Horace Doyle Barnette, November 24, 1964; by Special Agent Henry Rask and Special Agent James Wooten; MIBURN files, p. 3

. . . "I thought you were going back to Meridian . . ." FBI signed statement of Horace Doyle Barnette, MIBURN files, p. 3

"There was nothing masochistic about Mickey. . . ." *Three Lives for Mississippi*, pp. 117–18

"I followed Price down Highway 19, and he turned left on to a gravel road . . ." FBI signed statement of Horace Doyle Barnette, MIBURN files, pp. 5–6

"Ashes to ashes, dust to dust . . ." *Three Lives for Mississippi*, p. 118

. . . Olen Burrage then led the group . . . FBI signed statement of Horace Doyle Barnette, MIBURN files, p. 7

At around 2:00 a.m. on Monday, June 22 . . . FBI signed statement of Horace Doyle Barnette, MIBURN files, p. 8

CHAPTER 2: ANDREW GOODMAN

"How dismally the day . . ." Andrew Goodman: 1943–1964, Eulogies Delivered at the Funeral Service of Andrew Goodman, August 9, 1964, at the Meetinghouse of the Society for Ethical Culture; David Goodman archive

On a summer day . . . *Back to Mississippi*, pp. 246–47

He hired one of the first black lawyers . . . David Goodman interview, February 1, 2012, Upper Saddle River, New Jersey

Carolyn obtained a degree from Cornell . . . *New York Times*, August 18, 2007, "Carolyn Goodman, Rights Champion, Dies at

91," by Margalit Fox; *Cornell Alumni Magazine*, November 15, 2007, "Letter from Ithaca: Mother Courage," by Brad Herzog

Robert, or Bobby as he was known . . . David Goodman interview

. . . **"that rare mixture . . ."** *New York Times*, May 21, 1969, "Robert W. Goodman, President of Pacifica Foundation, Is Dead"

Charles Goodman was responsible . . . *New York Times*, December 5, 1963, "Charles Goodman Dies at 79; Head of Grow Construction Co."

He cared less about money . . . David Goodman interview

"Grandpa Goodman had a profound impact . . ." *Back to Mississippi*, p. 250

"It's clear as a bell" . . . David Goodman interview

David characterized his parents . . . David Goodman interview

"Be a doer." David Goodman interview

"He only showed respect . . ." David Goodman interview

"We got out of line . . ." David Goodman interview

When he helped Andy and his brothers . . . David Goodman interview

"he played on the street . . ." Carolyn Goodman, "Andrew Goodman: 1943–1964" in *Freedom Is a Constant Struggle: An Anthology of the Mississippi Civil Rights Movement*, p. 320

". . . in our family, nobody bullied him. . . ." David Goodman interview

. . . **two upperclassmen were picking on him.** David Goodman interview

The school placed a premium on tailoring education . . . *We Are Not Afraid*, pp. 52–53

. . . **"come up with your understanding of the way the world is . . ."** David Goodman interview

Carolyn, Jonathan, and David were the "street smart" members of the family. . . . David Goodman interview

Andy and his brothers took music classes at the Juilliard School . . . David Goodman interview

Jackie Robinson, who became . . . Carolyn Goodman, "Andrew Goodman: 1943–1964" in *Freedom Is a Constant Struggle: An Anthology of the Mississippi Civil Rights Movement*, p. 321

He recalled an incident when Andy was in the sixth grade. *Children and Dramatics*, pp. 265–266

Andy was particularly close to his cousin Jane Mark. Jane Mark telephone interview, March 10, 2012

"Andy was like my brother." Jane Mark telephone interview

Andy had "an intellectually serious side" . . . Ralph Engelman interview, February 2, 2012, Brooklyn, New York

"[o]ne of the things I liked best about Andy . . ." Booklet of eulogies for Andrew Goodman, David Goodman archives

"Books mattered . . ." Ralph Engelman interview

"Andy was one of those rare individuals . . ." Ralph Engelman interview

Coming to Walden was an adjustment for Ruth . . . Ruth Grunzweig Roth telephone interview, March 17, 2012

That's the context in which Andy and Ruth . . . Ruth Grunzweig Roth telephone interview

Their relationship intensified . . . Ruth Grunzweig Roth telephone interview

. . . involved in the nuclear disarmament peace movement. The National Committee for a Sane Nuclear Policy (SANE); Ralph Engelman interview

. . . a strong sense of cultural connection . . . Ralph Engelman interview

Andy sat next to a black man . . . *We Are Not Afraid*, p. 63

"That was an amazing experience. . . ." Ralph Engelman interview

"I think it just made more real . . ." Ralph Engelman interview, February 2, 2012, Brooklyn, New York

. . . in early 1960, the two young activists . . . *We Are Not Afraid*, p. 65

. . . "awareness that the problem of race . . ." Ralph Engelman interview

He returned home to New York City . . . *We Are Not Afraid*, p. 94

Andy demonstrated his strength . . . *Back to Mississippi*, p. 248

. . . "resented unfriendly acts . . ." *We Are Not Afraid*, p. 231

And his friend Ralph Engelman . . . Ralph Engelman interview

. . . they talked on the phone every Sunday . . . Ruth Grunzweig Roth telephone interview

Andy "was not going to go against . . ." Ruth Grunzweig Roth telephone interview

. . . "a very real desire to help . . ." Aaron Henry letter to Goodman family, August 15, 1964; David Goodman archive

"I, of course, would gladly . . ." *Three Lives for Mississippi*, p. 91

. . . the Goodmans held a going-away party . . . Jane Mark telephone interview

. . . on Malcolm X and the Black Muslim movement. Andrew Goodman, "Term Paper: The Black Muslims." Sociology 21E, Dr. Elizabeth K. Nottingham, Queens College, New York, May 19, 1964, p. 29; David Goodman archives

Jane thought the paper "astonishing. . . ." Jane Mark telephone interview

Andy waited for one evening over dinner . . . *We Are Not Afraid*, p. 243

Andy, she said, "felt it was unfair . . ." *Three Lives for Mississippi*, pp. 90–91

Jane Mark's father . . . Jane Mark telephone interview

The night before Andy left . . . Ruth Grunzweig Roth telephone interview

The following morning, Bobby Goodman woke up . . . Documentary film *Neshoba: The Price of Freedom*

CHAPTER 3: JAMES CHANEY

. . . an enterprising black man named James Chapel . . . *We Are Not Afraid*, p. 165; Ben Chaney, "They Came Up Missing" in *Freedom Is a Constant Struggle: An Anthology of the Mississippi Civil Rights Movement*, p. 329

She became Fannie Lee Chaney . . . *We Are Not Afraid*, p. 162

. . . Fannie Lee went to work as a domestic servant . . . *We Are Not Afraid*, p. 163

They worked hard to pay the tuition . . . *We Are Not Afraid*, p. 163

Fannie Lee was "an absolutely awesome individual . . ." Julia Chaney-Moss telephone interview, April 1, 2012

. . . Fannie Lee came to depend on her two oldest children . . . Julia Chaney-Moss telephone interview

. . . James was "willing to allow Barbara Jean to be the heavy . . ." Julia Chaney-Moss telephone interview

His sister Julia remembers J.E. as "a fun-loving character. . . ." Julia Chaney-Moss telephone interview

David Sims, who grew up next door . . . *New York Times*, June 20, 2005, "Rights Workers Honored as Trial in Their Killings Proceeds," by Shaila Dewan

Roscoe Jones remembers James . . . Roscoe Jones interview

Church was always important . . . Julia Chaney-Moss telephone interview

Despite being somewhat small and severely asthmatic . . . Julia Chaney-Moss telephone interview

Once, when he was in high school . . . *We Are Not Afraid*, p. 166

. . . mother and son regularly stayed up late . . . *We Are Not Afraid*, p. 166

"We never had [a conversation] because parenting in the South . . ." Julia Chaney-Moss telephone interview

When the Chaneys' eldest child, Barbara, was twelve years old . . . *We Are Not Afraid*, p. 164

"We lived across the street from a white family. . . ." *Freedom's Children*, p. 4

James went to Harris Junior College . . . *We Are Not Afraid*, pp. 166–167

The school's principal was not sympathetic. . . . Julia Chaney-Moss telephone interview

The principal undoubtedly saw what James did not see . . . Julia Chaney-Moss telephone interview

James attempted to join the military . . . Julia Chaney-Moss telephone interview

He was able to observe the political hierarchies . . . Julia Chaney-Moss telephone interview

In 1962, Ben Chaney Sr. earned enough money . . . *We Are Not Afraid*, p. 170

. . . James would serve as Suarez's primary assistant . . . *We Are Not Afraid*, p. 252

James regularly canvassed black ministers . . . Julia Chaney-Moss telephone interview

He then went off to help Matt Suarez . . . *We Are Not Afraid*, p. 270

All of James's civil rights work, both prior to working with . . . Julia Chaney-Moss telephone interview

. . . the Schwerners were "in and out of our house . . ." Julia Chaney-Moss telephone interview

Julia fondly remembers the Schwerners as "a wonderful couple. . . ." Julia Chaney-Moss telephone interview

In April 1964, they wrote national headquarters . . . *We Are Not Afraid*, p. 271

James embraced the civil rights movement's use of nonviolence. Julia Chaney-Moss telephone interview

James's father was concerned about the risks . . . Julia Chaney-Moss telephone interview

. . . Julia recalled that "we would turn the lights off . . ." Julia Chaney-Moss telephone interview

His sister Julia recalled, "And for him it was not escaping the risk . . ." Julia Chaney-Moss telephone interview

Young Ben Chaney would become active . . . *Clarion-Ledger*, June 14, 2005, "Neshoba Slayings: Mississippi's Past on Trial — KKK wizard greets Killen as trial unfolds in slayings," by Jerry Mitchell

"My mother was okay with that to some degree . . ." Julia Chaney-Moss telephone interview

. . . "[w]hatever my brother wanted to do . . ." *Freedom's Children*, p. 101

"It was okay to be hit. . . ." *Freedom's Children*, pp. 102–03

CHAPTER 4: MICHAEL SCHWERNER

"One day . . . you might find something worth dying for. . . ." *Freedom's Children*, p. 105

. . . when Mickey Schwerner was eighteen and getting ready to leave his home . . . *Three Lives for Mississippi*, p. 9

. . . or Mickey as he was known . . . *We Are Not Afraid*, p. 256

"We grew up in a family that believed in social justice. . . ." *Yellow Springs News*, January 13, 2005, "Schwerner Says Questions Remain Unanswered in Slaying of Brother," by Diane Chiddister

Both Mickey and his brother loved sports . . . *We Are Not Afraid*, p. 256

"Perhaps he believed so tenaciously in Man . . ." *Three Lives for Mississippi*, pp. 31–32

Mickey spent his freshman year of college at Michigan State University . . . *We Are Not Afraid*, p. 257

When Mickey was home at Pelham in the summer . . . *We Are Not Afraid*, p. 257

Mickey was impatient for action in the area of civil rights . . . *New York Times*, August 6, 1964, "Families of Rights Workers Voice Grief and Hope," by Philip Benjamin

So in June 1962, Mickey left school . . . *We Are Not Afraid*, pp. 257–58

A caring person . . . *We Are Not Afraid*, p. 258

Mickey came to view social work . . . *We Are Not Afraid*, p. 258

On July 4, 1963, Mickey joined a CORE-sponsored sit-in . . . *We Are Not Afraid*, p. 259; *New York Times*, July 25, 1963, "5 Racial Pickets Here Get 30-to-60-Day Jail Terms," by Peter Kihss

"I am now so thoroughly identified with the civil rights struggle . . ." *We Are Not Afraid*, p. 259

. . . it was her hope to "someday pass on to the children . . ." *We Are Not Afraid*, p. 259

The Schwerners received word . . . *We Are Not Afraid*, p. 260

Mickey was "a little short guy . . ." Roscoe Jones interview

The affable Mickey fit in well . . . *We Are Not Afraid*, p. 260

When they first arrived in Meridian . . . *Mississippi Black Paper*, p. 59

By the end of February 1964, Meridian's community center . . . *We Are Not Afraid*, pp. 261–62

Larry Martin was a frequent visitor . . . *Freedom's Children*, p. 96

"James was a nice, easygoing fella . . ." *Freedom's Children*, p. 96

"Now don't think that Mickey came to the South green. . . ." Julia Chaney-Moss telephone interview

. . . "it was great to see them chatting and laughing . . ." Julia Chaney-Moss telephone interview

The couple recruited Sue Brown . . . *We Are Not Afraid*, p. 262

. . . "[b]y May we received so many phone calls . . ." *Mississippi Black Paper*, p. 60

. . . "such as someone calling and telling me . . ." *Mississippi Black Paper*, p. 60

A store owner close to the center . . . *Mississippi Black Paper*, p. 60

On the first Sunday in March 1964 . . . *We Are Not Afraid*, p. 267

By at least March 1964 . . . Sovereignty Commission file; Supplementary Offense Report, Meridian Police Department, March 19, 1964, by G. L. Butler

In a Sovereignty Commission report, a commission investigator stated . . . Sovereignty Commission file; "Investigation of Unknown White Male CORE Worker at Meridian, Mississippi"; March 23, 1964, by A. L. Hopkins, Investigator

With James Chaney's assistance, Mickey was able . . . *We Are Not Afraid*, p. 271

. . . the two adhered to a rigid security protocol . . . *Mississippi Black Paper*, p. 61

Once, Rita asked to accompany the two men . . . *Mississippi Black Paper*, p. 62

. . . Mickey moved forward with an ambitious plan . . . *We Are Not Afraid*, p. 273

. . . but he was placed in a cell with white prisoners. *We Are Not Afraid*, p. 274

"You must be that Communist-Jew . . ." *We Are Not Afraid*, p. 274

Unbeknownst to Mickey, in March 1964 . . . November 7, 1964, memo from Jackson, Mississippi, Special Agent in Charge Joseph Sullivan to FBI Director J. Edgar Hoover; MIBURN files; excerpt of memo references interview with Delmar Dennis, a twenty-four-year-old Methodist minister who joined the White Knights of the Ku Klux Klan of Mississippi on March 26, 1964.

CHAPTER 5: THE LONG SUMMER

"You don't know the Deep South like I do. . . ." "Deacon Summer" in *Don't Quit Your Day Job*, pp. 59–75

Fannie Lee Chaney was worried. Julia Chaney-Moss telephone interview

David Goodman woke up early on Monday, June 22 . . . David Goodman interview

Rita Schwerner was awakened in her dorm room . . . *Three Lives for Mississippi*, p. 127

At Oxford, Bob Moses addressed the next group . . . *We Are Not Afraid*, p. 320

"And then she left, and she was very emotional . . ." *Voices of Freedom*, p. 190

"Farmer, don't go over there. . . ." *Lay Bare the Heart*, p. 273

Lewis recalled that the town square "looked like an armed camp. . . ." *Walking with the Wind*, p. 257

"Rainey and Price did nothing to hide their contempt for us. . . ." *Walking with the Wind*, p. 257

The *New York Times*'s first story on the case . . . *New York Times*, June 23, 1964, "3 in Rights Drive Reported Missing: Mississippi Campaign Heads Fear Foul Play — Inquiry by F.B.I. is Ordered," by Claude Sitton

"If you were a nigger . . ." *Witness in Philadelphia*, pp. 92–93

Etched in his memory is the last time . . . Stanley Dearman interview, June 3, 2012, Philadelphia, Mississippi

Dearman arrived at the newspaper at 6:00 a.m. on the morning . . . Stanley Dearman interview

Johnson asked him what he thought happened . . . *The Presidential Recordings*, p. 52

"Now, I'm going to tell you . . ." *The Presidential Recordings*, p. 60

Eastland later asked, "Who would . . . could possibly harm them?" *The Presidential Recordings*, p. 62

Yet Neshoba County was well-known as being particularly hostile . . . Documentary film *Neshoba: The Price of Freedom*

Eastland's view that the disappearance of the three men . . . *The Presidential Recordings*, pp. 64–65

In response, Johnson suggested the possibility . . . *The Presidential Recordings*, p. 65

Late that same afternoon on June 23 . . . *The Presidential Recordings*, pp. 85–91

That evening, the president received word . . . *The Presidential Recordings*, p. 136

In a conversation with Hoover the next day . . . *The Presidential Recordings*, p. 154

In the days and weeks to come, military personnel were enlisted . . . *The Presidential Recordings*, p. 245

On June 25, President Johnson authorized the deployment . . . *New York Times*, June 26, 1964; "President Sends 200 Sailors to Aid Mississippi Hunt: Force Is Unarmed: Governor Is Agreeable to Help in Finding 3 Rights Workers"

They were at the Cincinnati airport . . . *New York Times*, June 17, 2005, "Widow Recalls Ghosts of '64 at Rights Trial," by Shaila Dewan

. . . Mississippi's new governor, Paul B. Johnson Jr., an avowed segregationist . . . *Three Lives for Mississippi*, p. 22

While Dulles was sensitive to Hoover's concerns . . . *Pillar of Fire*, p. 368

At the conclusion of the meeting, Dulles extended his sympathy . . . *New York Times*, June 26, 1964, "Dulles Gets Plea to Send Marshals," by David Halberstam

When Rita and Zellner arrived at the Philadelphia motel . . . *We Are Not Afraid*, pp. 360–61

Rainey told Rita and her companion . . . *Mississippi Black Paper*, p. 63

As they drove away from Philadelphia . . . *We Are Not Afraid*, p. 361

. . . "not even the local government acknowledged my mother." Julia Chaney-Moss telephone interview

Julia recalls that not only did the state and local officials . . . Julia Chaney-Moss telephone interview

. . . she spent a great deal of her time walking "from window to door . . ." Julia Chaney-Moss, documentary film *Neshoba: The Price of Freedom*

She often cleaned the house incessantly . . . Ben Chaney, "They Came Up Missing," in *Freedom Is a Constant Struggle: An Anthology of the Mississippi Civil Rights Movement*, pp. 328–29

"I think that my mother believed that my brother and the others were dead. . . ." *Freedom's Children*, p. 103

"I was sure he'd be found, because I admired him so much . . ." *Los Angeles Times*, June 15, 1989, "A Burning Legacy: 25 Years Ago This Summer, 3 Murders in Mississippi Sparked a Revolution in Civil Rights, a Fire the Victims' Families and Activists Hope to Rekindle," by Josh Getlin

The Chaneys were also surprised to learn that summer . . .

Julia Chaney-Moss telephone interview; *We Are Not Afraid*, p. 368; *People*, January 9, 1989, "Since Mississippi Burned," by Diane McWhorter

On June 29, Rita and Congressman Ogden Reid . . . *The Presidential Recordings*, p. 273 and footnote

. . . he had met with Rita, who "wants thousands of extra people . . ." *The Presidential Recordings*, p. 274

Hoover told the president during this same conversation . . . *The Presidential Recordings*, p. 275. The FBI opened a field office in Jackson, Mississippi, on July 10.

After her meeting with President Johnson . . . *New York Times*, June 30, 1964, "Mrs. Schwerner Sees Johnson"

"This is a strange, tight little town. . . ." *Life*, December 18, 1964, "A Strange, Tight Little Town, Loath to Admit Complicity," by David Nevin, p. 38

On July 24, 1964, Dr. Martin Luther King Jr. . . . *Pillar of Fire*, pp. 414–15

Jewel Rush McDonald grew up in Neshoba County . . . Jewel Rush McDonald interview

As the Rush family lived out in the country . . . Jewel Rush McDonald interview

Sheriff Lawrence Rainey and Deputy Sheriff Cecil Price enjoyed exercising their power . . . Dick Molpus interview, June 3, 2012, Jackson, Mississippi

In 1963, Rainey was elected sheriff. July 15, 1964, memorandum from FBI Special Agent John P. Slayden and Special Assistant Lawrence D. Kennedy to SAC New Orleans

It was already well-known that Rainey had killed two black men . . . *Life*, December 18, 1964, "A Strange, Tight Little Town, Loath to Admit Complicity" by David Nevin, p. 38

Jewel Rush, who lived in the country outside Philadelphia . . . Jewel Rush McDonald interview

The bullying behavior of Sheriff Rainey and Deputy Sheriff Price . . . Jewel Rush McDonald interview

Not everyone in Neshoba County's white community . . . *We Are Not Afraid*, p. 346

Posey recalled immediately after the murders . . . Documentary film *Neshoba: The Price of Freedom*

Her grandfather owned a great deal of property . . . Stanley Dearman interview

CHAPTER 6: THREE STREAKS OF LIGHTNING IN THE SKY

"[W]hen people die on a cross, they sacrifice. . . ." Florence Mars interview with the University of Southern Mississippi Center for Oral History & Cultural Heritage, January 5, 1978

Larry Martin spent a great deal of time . . . *Freedom's Children*, p. 100

An informant finally provided the information . . . FBI memo dated August 12, 1964, recording measurements of earthen dam taken at Old Jolly Farm, Neshoba County, Mississippi, on August 5, 1964; authors' names redacted; MIBURN files

A bulldozer and other excavation equipment . . . *We Are Not Afraid*, pp. 396–400

. . . "[t]he left hand of this body was clenched in a tight fist. . . ." FBI memorandum dated August 12, 1964, regarding the August 4 exhumation of James Chaney, Andrew Goodman, and Michael Schwerner from the earthen dam at the Old Jolly Farm, Neshoba County, Mississippi; names of FBI Special Agent authors redacted; MIBURN files

Ruth Grunzweig was horrified to learn this fact . . . Ruth Grunzweig Roth telephone interview

Shortly after 8:00 p.m. President Johnson received a phone call . . . *The Presidential Recordings of Lyndon B. Johnson*, Digital

Edition; WH6408-05-4693, August 4, 1964; University of Virginia Miller Center for Public Affairs

"The Goodman family are out at the theater, but I got their son, an eighteen-year old boy [David Goodman]..." *The Presidential Recordings of Lyndon B. Johnson,* Digital Edition; WH6408-06-4701, August 4, 1964; University of Virginia Miller Center for Public Affairs. David Goodman was actually seventeen years old at the time of his brother's death; he turned eighteen years old in October 1964. November 25, 2012, David Goodman e-mail to author

"And the Schwerners themselves, the parents of the boy who was missing..." *The Presidential Recordings of Lyndon B. Johnson,* Digital Edition; WH6408-06-4701, August 4, 1964; University of Virginia Miller Center for Public Affairs

The FBI had specifically requested that Cecil Price... *We Are Not Afraid,* p. 400

Later that evening, DeLoach and President Johnson spoke again... *The Presidential Recordings of Lyndon B. Johnson,* Digital Edition; WH6408-06-4713, August 4, 1964; University of Virginia Miller Center for Public Affairs

The lengthy autopsy showed that both Mickey and Andy had each been shot once... FBI memorandum dated August 12, 1964, regarding the August 5 autopsies of James Chaney, Andrew Goodman, and Michael Schwerner in Jackson, Mississippi; Special Agent Jay Cochran Jr. and Special Agent Anthony O'Tousa; MIBURN files

Because of the advanced state of decomposition, the pathologist stated... FBI memorandum dated August 11, 1964, from Special Agent in Charge, Jackson, Mississippi, to FBI Director regarding the August 5 autopsies of James Chaney, Andrew Goodman, and Michael Schwerner in Jackson, Mississippi; MIBURN files

... "the lower jaw was completely shattered . . ." Dr. David M. Spain, "Mississippi Autopsy" in *Mississippi Eyewitness: The Three Civil Rights Workers — How They Were Murdered*, p. 49

"Pete Seeger announced that the bodies had been found. . . ." Roscoe Jones interview

Ralph Engelman was working at a newspaper in Michigan. . . . Ralph Engelman interview

It was the first time the couple had gone out socially . . . *We Are Not Afraid*, p. 402; November 25, 2012 David Goodman e-mail to author

During the performance, a family friend appeared in the aisle . . . *We Are Not Afraid*, p. 402

Andy Goodman was well-known at this camp . . . Jane Mark telephone interview

Hoover replied, "We have the names of the people . . ." *The Presidential Recordings of Lyndon B. Johnson*, Digital Edition; WH6408-05-4760, August 5, 1964; University of Virginia Miller Center for Public Affairs

... "I want my brother! . . ." *We Are Not Afraid*, pp. 408–09

Roscoe Jones recalled Meridian being "bombarded with people" . . . Roscoe Jones interview

"So I just stopped and said what I felt. . . ." *Eyes on the Prize*, pp. 238–40

When Carolyn came into the hall . . . *Back to Mississippi*, p. 252

... "[o]n the eve of his departure for Oxford, Ohio, Andy . . ." *We Are Not Afraid*, pp. 410–11; Booklet of eulogies for Andrew Goodman, David Goodman archives

At the conclusion of Andy's memorial service . . . *We Are Not Afraid*, p. 411

Andy's cousin Jane Mark walked outside . . . Jane Mark telephone interview

The Schwerners attempted to have Mickey buried . . . *We Are*

Not Afraid, p. 408; *New York Times*, August 10, 1964, "Slain Rights Workers Mourned by Thousands at Service Here," by John Sibley

"Beyond the immediacy of our grief . . ." *My Life as a Radical Lawyer*, p. 142

Carmichael indicated that this was the seventeenth funeral he'd been to . . . Stephen Schwerner interview, February 2, 2012, New York, New York

"The tragedy has become a symbol . . ." *New York Times*, August 7, 1964, "Mississippi Rights Slaying Is Being Reconstructed — Arrests Awaited," by Claude Sitton

. . . "And I want us all to stand up here together . . ." *Three Lives for Mississippi*, p. 146

"After I made that speech, my father gave me a hard time. . . ." *Freedom's Children*, p. 104

. . . Ella Baker stated that "[u]ntil the killing of a black mother's son . . ." *New York Times*, August 7, 1964; "Mississippi Rights Slaying Is Being Reconstructed — Arrests Awaited," by Claude Sitton

. . . "in Philadelphia, Mississippi, young people seeking to secure . . ." http://www.nobelprize.org/nobel_prizes/peace/laureates/1964/king-acceptance_en.html

CHAPTER 7: MAKING THE FEDERAL CASE

"Neshoba County juries rarely convicted a white man . . ." *Witness in Philadelphia*, p. 17

Unless committed on federal property, murder is a violation of state law . . . *New York Times*, October 10, 1967, "All-White Jury Picked as Trial of 18 in Slaying of 3 Rights Workers Begins in Mississippi," by Walter Rugaber

On December 4, 1964, four months to the day . . . December 4, 1964, FBI press release Jackson, Mississippi; MIBURN files

On December 10, the accused men... *We Are Not Afraid*, p. 437

However, on February 24, 1965, Cox dismissed the felony charges... *Federal Law and Southern Order*, p. 169

The matter was appealed to the US Supreme Court... *Federal Law and Southern Order*, pp. 159–82

On June 21, 1966, King and Ralph Abernathy came to Philadelphia, Mississippi... *Witness in Philadelphia*, p. 207

Young Dick Molpus had been admonished by his mother... Dick Molpus interview

Encountering Deputy Sheriff Cecil Price, King addressed the crowd... *At Canaan's Edge*, p. 488

A voice close to Cecil Price replied... Dick Molpus interview

..."They ought to search their hearts...." *Witness in Philadelphia*, p. 209

As King led the marchers out of town, the confrontation burst into violence... *Witness in Philadelphia*, pp. 209–10

"This is a terrible town, the worst I've seen...." *We Are Not Afraid*, p. 382

...a new grand jury reindicted the conspirators on February 28, 1967. *We Are Not Afraid*, p. 443

At last, the federal trial began in Meridian, Mississippi... *We Are Not Afraid*, p. 446

He also asked Reverend Johnson if he "and Mr. Schwerner didn't advocate..." *United States v. Cecil Ray Price et. al.*, October 9, 1967, trial transcript, pp. 113–16

For instance, Meridian policeman Sergeant Carlton Wallace Miller testified... *New York Times*, October 12, 1967, "Informer Links Klan to Rights Slayings," by Walter Rugaber

...Reverend Delmar Dennis testified that Ku Klux Klan Imperial Wizard Sam Bowers... *New York Times*, October

12, 1967, "Informer Links Klan to Rights Slayings," by Walter Rugaber

"Members of the jury, this is an important case. . . ." *United States v. Cecil Ray Price et. al.*, October 18, 1967, trial transcript, pp. 2,363–364

Later that day, Judge Cox directed the jury . . . *We Are Not Afraid*, p. 450

. . . "a sigh came from a woman in the crowd believed to be Price's wife." *Eyes on Mississippi*, p. 238

The clerk quickly corrected herself and continued . . . *United States v. Cecil Ray Price et. al.*, October 20, 1967, trial transcript, p. 2,548

Minor reported that "Price's wife put her hand to her throat . . ." *Eyes on Mississippi*, p. 238

In addition to Cecil Price and Jimmy Arledge . . . *We Are Not Afraid*, pp. 450–51

The convicted defendants were sentenced by Judge Cox . . . *New York Times*, January 14, 1968, "Witness Gets Jail in Rights Killings"

Judge Cox later stated that "[t]hey killed one nigger, one Jew . . ." *We Are Not Afraid*, p. 452

The convicted men served time in prison . . . *We Are Not Afraid*, p. 456

In 1999, Alton Wayne Roberts died of heart trouble. *Clarion-Ledger*, September 14, 1999, "Klansman in 1960s slayings case dies: Effort to reopen triple murder case debated," by Jerry Mitchell

Lawrence Rainey, who was acquitted in the case . . . *New York Times*, November 13, 2002, "Lawrence Rainey, 79, a Rights-Era Suspect," by David Stout

. . . "If nobody had paid those boys any mind . . ." *We Are Not Afraid*, p. 457

CHAPTER 8: MISSISSIPPI MOVES TOWARD A MURDER TRIAL

Mississippi Moves Toward a Murder Trial: "I believed at the time . . ." Rita (Schwerner) Bender, "Comments Upon Twenty-Fifth Anniversary Commemoration At Statuary Hall, U.S. Congress, June 23, 1989" in *Freedom Is a Constant Struggle: An Anthology of the Mississippi Civil Rights Movement*, ed. Susie Erenrich (Montgomery: Black Belt Press, 1999) p. 415

Life in Meridian became increasingly difficult for the Chaney family . . . *New York Times*, May 24, 1970, "A Young Militant's Path to Prison," by Charlayne Hunter

Fannie Lee was not able to find another job. Julia Chaney-Moss telephone interview

Julia Chaney would later move up to the New York City area . . . Julia Chaney-Moss telephone interview

He also traveled with his mother and spoke extensively on civil rights . . . *New York Times*, May 24, 1970, "A Young Militant's Path to Prison," by Charlayne Hunter

Ben's interest in the Walden School waned . . . *Los Angeles Times*, June 15, 1989, "A Burning Legacy: 25 Years Ago This Summer, 3 Murders in Mississippi Sparked a Revolution in Civil Rights, a Fire the Victims' Families and Activists Hope to Rekindle," by Josh Getlin; *Smithsonian*, December 2008, "The Lasting Impact of a Civil Rights Icon's Murder," by Hank Klibanoff

. . . established the James Earl Chaney Foundation. James Earl Chaney Foundation website, http://www.jecf.org/wordpress-site/

On June 20, 1965, the Goodmans held a ceremony at Andy's gravesite . . . Letter dated July 9, 1965, from Carolyn Goodman to Mary Travers of Peter, Paul and Mary; David Goodman archive

With the death of their son . . . Andrew Goodman Foundation website, http://www.andrewgoodman.org

Andy's father, Robert, died of a stroke . . . *New York Times*, May 21, 1969, "Robert W. Goodman, President of Pacifica Foundation, Is Dead: Father of Rights Aide Slain in Mississippi Was Head of a Construction Company"; Jane Mark telephone interview

Carolyn later remarried, and she would be widowed a second time . . . Memorial brochure for life of Dr. Carolyn Goodman, October 6, 1915–August 17, 2007; David Goodman archive

Mickey's parents, Anne and Nathan Schwerner, went on to raise funds . . . *New York Times*, June 20, 1965, "Families Hope 3 Didn't Die in Vain: Feel Rights Workers' Deaths Stirred an Awareness," by Philip Benjamin

Nathan Schwerner died in 1991 . . . *New York Times*, March 7, 1991, "Nathan Schwerner, 80, Rights Worker's Father"

Anne Schwerner, a retired high school biology teacher . . . *New York Times*, December 4, 1996, "Anne Schwerner, Civil Rights Worker's Mother, 84"

One federal government report in March 1971 . . . *New York Times*, March 4, 1971, "Philadelphia, Miss., Erasing Memories of Violence," by Roy Reed

Fenton DeWeese, a white attorney with historic family ties . . . Fenton DeWeese interview, June 5, 2012, Choctaw, Mississippi

In 1975, a two-part television docudrama . . . Entitled *Attack on Terror: The FBI versus the Ku Klux Klan* starred Ned Beatty, Dabney Coleman, George Grizzard, Rip Torn, and Wayne Rogers, and was based on a book by Don Whitehead.

"I believe in states' rights" and that as president he pledged . . . *The Neshoba Democrat*, August 1980

Mickey's brother, Steve Schwerner, observed that Reagan . . ." Stephen Schwerner interview

Stanley Dearman moved to Neshoba County as a young man . . . Stanley Dearman interview

After his stint at the *Meridian Star*, he came to Philadelphia . . . Stanley Dearman interview. Dearman stayed with the *Neshoba Democrat* until August 2000.

This treatment of the black community "had become second nature . . ." Stanley Dearman interview

Stanley Dearman referred to these as the "years of futility." Stanley Dearman interview

Stanley Dearman recalled that "the major industries around town . . ." Stanley Dearman interview

The interview had "a profound effect" . . . Stanley Dearman interview

Mickey's brother, Steve Schwerner, found the twenty-fifth anniversary . . . Stephen Schwerner interview

Andy's friend Ralph Engelman said at the event . . . *New York Times*, June 22, 1989, "Mississippi Anniversary Recalls Lessons in Blood" by Peter Applebome

With the twenty-fifth anniversary of the triple murders approaching . . . Dick Molpus interview

"We deeply regret what happened here twenty-five years ago. . . ." Remarks by Secretary of State Dick Molpus, Ecumenical Memorial Service, Mount Zion Methodist Church, June 21, 1989; Philadelphia Coalition website, http://www.neshobajustice.com /pages/molpus89.htm

"It was a brave thing for him to do" . . . Stanley Dearman interview

Molpus recalled: "I got an enormous response . . ." Dick Molpus interview

The twenty-fifth anniversary built up momentum . . . Stanley Dearman interview

However, the apology also got Molpus a number of death threats . . . Dick Molpus interview

Mitchell attended a screening of the film . . . Jerry Mitchell interview, June 4, 2012, Brandon, Mississippi

In 1990, another television film dramatizing the case, *Murder in Mississippi*, was televised nationally . . . The TV movie *Murder in Mississippi* starred Tom Hulce, Blair Underwood, and Jennifer Grey.

. . . as Mitchell continued to write about this . . . Jerry Mitchell interview

. . . in 1998, Bowers would finally be convicted and sentenced to life in prison . . . *New York Times*, November 6, 2006, "Samuel Bowers, 82, Klan Leader Convicted in Fatal Bombing, Dies," by Jennifer 8. Lee

In January 1984, Bowers had given an oral-history interview . . . Interview with Sam H. Bowers Jr. by Debra Spencer in Florence, Mississippi, January 30, 1984, Mississippi Department of Archives and History. Bowers died on November 6, 2006, in the Mississippi State Penitentiary at Parchman.

Jerry Mitchell uncovered and reported on this interview . . . *Clarion-Ledger*, December 27, 1998, "Bowers: Klansman got away with murder," by Jerry Mitchell

Early in 1999, Mississippi attorney general Michael Moore reopened the case . . . *New York Times*, June 12, 2005, "Revisiting '64 Civil Rights Deaths, This Time in a Murder Trial," by Shaila Dewan

In May 2001, Cecil Price died . . . *New York Times*, May 9, 2001, "Cecil Price, 63, Deputy Guilty in Killing of 3 Rights Workers," by David Stout

"This is a case that never goes away . . ." *The Neshoba Democrat*, May 3, 2000, "June 21, 1964: It's time for an accounting," by Stanley Dearman

In 2004, Dick Molpus, now retired from public office ... Dick Molpus interview

While racial reconciliation was an important part ... Fenton DeWeese interview

In May 2004, the Philadelphia Coalition held a press conference ... Philadelphia Coalition website, http://www.neshobajustice .com/pages/2004mem.htm

In Jerry Mitchell's view, the successful effort ... Jerry Mitchell interview and Dick Molpus interview

... Attorney General Jim Hood met with the Philadelphia Coalition ... *Clarion-Ledger*, January 9, 2005, "As Crime Victim, Hood Understands Wanting Justice," by Jerry Mitchell

It was an emotional session. Jewel Rush McDonald and Fenton DeWeese interview, June 5, 2012, Choctaw, Mississippi

Hood would not discuss the specifics of the investigation ... *Justice in Mississippi*, pp. 94–95

Prosecutors laid out before the grand jury ... *Clarion-Ledger*, January 7, 2005, "Grand jury indicts Killen in '64 killings," by Jerry Mitchell

As Attorney General Jim Hood stated ... *Clarion-Ledger*, January 8, 2005, "Killen Pleads Not Guilty in Civil Rights Killings," by Jerry Mitchell

CHAPTER 9: THE TRIAL OF EDGAR RAY KILLEN

"Who the hell [does] he think he is ..." Documentary film *Neshoba: The Price of Freedom*

Several years before Edgar Ray Killen was indicted ... *The New Yorker*, January 17, 2005, "Visiting Preacher Killen," by Jeffrey Goldberg

James Jordan had given testimony ... *New York Times*, October 13, 1967, "Witness Tells of Role in Slaying of Rights Workers," by Walter Rugaber

Jerry Mitchell later discovered . . . *Clarion-Ledger,* May 7, 2000, "Free," by Jerry Mitchell

As Stanley Dearman observed, "Edgar Ray Killen was the ringleader. . . ." Stanley Dearman interview

. . . "I don't really think among my neighbors . . ." Documentary film *Neshoba: The Price of Freedom*

Edgar Ray Killen had another run-in with the law in 1975 . . . *Clarion-Ledger,* May 1, 2005, "Experts: Killen Tape Could See Trial," by Jerry Mitchell; *Clarion-Ledger,* May 1, 2005, "Preacher Refused Plea Deal in '75," by Jerry Mitchell

Jerry Mitchell had talked to Edgar Ray Killen . . . Jerry Mitchell interview

The beginning of Edgar Ray Killen's trial was delayed . . . *Justice in Mississippi,* pp. 131–32

At the time of the 2005 trial, seven of the original defendants . . . *New York Times,* June 22, 2005, "Ex-Klansman Guilty of Manslaughter in 1964 Deaths," by Shaila Dewan

Joseph "Mike" Hatcher, a former Klansman . . . *Justice in Mississippi,* pp. 162–63

"You're treating this trial as the most important trial . . ." *New York Times,* June 17, 2005, "Widow Recalls Ghosts of '64 at Rights Trial," by Shaila Dewan

"I'd driven on all that red Mississippi dirt . . ." *New York Times,* June 24, 2005, "Closure, Or Something Close Enough," by Clyde Haberman

As her daughter Julia noted, "She lived for that moment." Julia Chaney-Moss telephone interview

The defense conceded to the jury that Edgar Ray Killen was a member of the Ku Klux Klan . . . *New York Times,* June 16, 2005, "A Klan Confession, but Not to 1964 Civil Rights Murders," by Shaila Dewan and Jerry Mitchell

"Is a Neshoba County jury going to tell the rest of the world . . ." *Justice in Mississippi*, p. 172

In Attorney General Jim Hood's closing argument . . . *Justice in Mississippi*, pp. 170–71

On June 21, 2005, forty-one years to the day . . . *Justice in Mississippi*, pp. 177–78

Murder means to kill someone with intent and malice aforethought . . . http://dictionary.law.com

. . . "The fact that some members of this jury could have sat through . . ." *New York Times*, June 22, 2005, "Ex-Klansman Guilty of Manslaughter in 1964 Deaths," by Shaila Dewan

She later commented, "[I]f he had gone for murder . . ." Jewel Rush McDonald interview

Neshoba County district attorney Mark Duncan stated, "We were asking a lot . . ." *Clarion-Ledger*, June 22, 2005, "Neshoba Slayings — The Verdict," by Jerry Mitchell

Two days after the jury returned its verdict . . . *New York Times*, June 24, 2005, "41 Years Later, Ex-Klansman Gets 60 Years in Civil Rights Deaths," by Ariel Hart

"She finally believes that the life of her son has some value . . ." *New York Times*, June 22, 2005, "Ex-Klansman Guilty of Manslaughter in 1964 Deaths," by Shaila Dewan

Fannie Lee Chaney died in February 2007 . . . *New York Times*, May 24, 2007, "Fannie Lee Chaney, 84, Mother of Slain Civil Rights Worker, Is Dead," by Douglas Martin

Later, in August of that year, Carolyn Goodman died . . . *New York Times*, August 18, 2007, "Carolyn Goodman, Rights Champion, Dies at 91," by Margalit Fox; *New York Times*, August 21, 2007, "A Life of Protest and Forgiveness," by Clyde Haberman

AFTERWORD: TOWARD THE BELOVED COMMUNITY

"I just hoped this case would go away and leave me alone. . . ." Stanley Dearman interview

. . . rooted in his conception of what he termed the Beloved Community . . . The King Center, www.thekingcenter.org/king-philosophy

Dr. King dreamed of a fully integrated society . . . *Search for the Beloved Community*, p. 130

"It woke up America," says Andy's brother . . . David Goodman interview

"In the great social movements in our country's history . . ." *New York Times*, June, 4, 2008, "Obama's Remarks at AIPAC"

"J.E., Mickey, and Andy did not die in vain" . . . Julia Chaney-Moss telephone interview

For Dick Molpus, the murder of the three men . . . Dick Molpus interview, June 3, 2012, Jackson, Mississippi

A milestone was reached in May 2009 when James Young was elected the first black mayor of Philadelphia . . . *New York Times*, May 21, 2009, "First Black Mayor in City Known for Klan Killings," by Robbie Brown

SAINT: FANNIE LOU HAMER

"Life was worse than hard" . . . *The Senator and the Sharecropper*, p. 53

"Sometimes when things were so bad . . ." *The Senator and the Sharecropper*, p. 53

At the age of six, Fannie . . . *This Little Light of Mine*, pp. 7–21

At the meeting, Hamer heard a number of civil rights activists . . . *We Are Not Afraid*, p. 187

"We are not ready for this in Mississippi." *Voices of Freedom*, p. 178

"But her deep religious faith . . ." *New York Times*, March 15, 1977, "Fannie Lou Hamer Dies; Left Farm to Lead Struggle for Civil Rights," by Thomas A. Johnson

"If we're trying to break down this barrier of segregation . . ." *The Senator and the Sharecropper*, p. 203

She taught the young people what to expect in Mississippi . . . *This Little Light of Mine*, p. 98

"A living example was Andy Goodman, James Chaney, and Michael Schwerner . . ." *This Little Light of Mine*, p. 307

VISIONARY: BOB MOSES

The police officer asked the young man . . . *And Gently He Shall Lead Them*, p. 46

Taken back to the police station, the unflappable civil rights worker . . . *And Gently He Shall Lead Them*, pp. 46–48

Robert Parris Moses was born in 1935 . . . *And Gently He Shall Lead Them*, pp. 11–16

"Before the Negro in the South had always looked . . ." *The Civil Rights Movement*, p. 71

Bob Moses came to this approach toward leadership naturally. *US News & World Report*, "The Civil Right to Radical Math," by Diane Cole, October 30, 2006, pp. 83–84; *Radical Equations*, p. 41

WITNESS: FLORENCE MARS

"You didn't wonder how she felt . . ." *Los Angeles Times*, April 30, 2006, "Florence Mars, 83; Assisted Probe of 1964 Klan Slayings," by Joceyln Y. Stewart

"I thought Negroes were supposed to be happy. . . ." *Witness in Philadelphia*, p. 15

She returned to Neshoba County in 1962 . . . *Witness in Philadelphia*, p. 41

Appalled at the murders committed in her county ...
Washington Post, April 30, 2006, "Florence Mars; Wrote of 1964
KKK Killings," by Joe Holley

Harassment against Mars came to a head ... *Witness in
Philadelphia*, p. 189

"I had been disdainful of Rainey ..." *Witness in Philadelphia*,
p. 191

The arrest of Florence Mars was a turning point ... Dick
Molpus interview

"Her book makes compelling reading; it should be in every
school ..." *New York Times*, September 10, 1977, "She Took Her
Stand in Dixie," by Richard R. Lingeman

Though confined to a wheelchair ... Fenton DeWeese
interview

"She was our conscience, our guide ..." *Los Angeles Times*,
April 30, 2006, "Florence Mars, 83; Assisted Probe of 1964 Klan
Slayings," by Joceyln Y. Stewart

INVESTIGATOR: JERRY MITCHELL

... it was "almost like it took place on another planet." Jerry
Mitchell interview

"I felt chills going down my spine. ..." *American Journalism
Review*, April/May 2005, "Out of the Past," by Sherry Ricchiardi

Bowers's first four trials for the Dahmer murder ... *New York
Times*, November 6, 2006, "Samuel Bowers, 82, Klan Leader
Convicted in Fatal Bombing, Dies," by Jennifer 8. Lee

... "by far the hardest case of the ones I've worked on ..."
Jerry Mitchell interview

"Edgar Ray Killen would not have been brought to justice ..."
Dick Molpus interview

The murders of James Chaney, Andrew Goodman, and Michael Schwerner was one of the most famous episodes of the American civil rights movement. Yet to the extent this story is covered in history books, it tends to be bounded by the day of their murder to the discovery of their bodies forty-four days later. There often seems to be little more of a profile offered of the three men than the grainy, posed photographs of them on the famous FBI MISSING poster from the summer of 1964. This book is an attempt to address this shortcoming, to tell their stories more fully and explore what made these three young men such caring individuals, how they became involved in the fight for civil rights, and how their sacrifice affected Neshoba County, the state of Mississippi, and the nation.

Accordingly, the most valuable part of my research, which took me to New York, New Jersey, and Mississippi, was interviewing individuals who knew James Chaney, Andrew Goodman, and Michael Schwerner, as well as others whose lives were impacted by the Freedom Summer murders. This is their story as well. I'm deeply grateful for the kindness and generosity of the following individuals who took the time to share their memories and insights: Julia Chaney-Moss, Stanley Dearman, Fenton B. DeWeese II, Ralph Engelman, David Goodman, Roscoe Jones Sr., Jane Mark, Jewel Rush McDonald, Jerry Mitchell (no relation to the author), Dick Molpus, Ruth Grunzweig Roth, and Stephen Schwerner. All of the individuals I interviewed reviewed an early draft of this manuscript. However, any errors contained in this book are solely my responsibility.

Readers can learn more about how the legacy of the three men has been perpetuated by accessing the Andrew Goodman Foundation at www.andrewgoodman.org as well as the James Earl Chaney Foundation at www.jecf.org. The Andrew Goodman archive is located at the Schomburg Center for Research in Black Culture in New York, New York.

Between 1963 and 1969, Lyndon Johnson secretly recorded approximately eight hundred hours of conversations while he was president of the United States, most of which were telephone conversations. The University of Virginia's Miller Center for Public Affairs' Presidential Recordings Program, in coordination with the Johnson Presidential Library, has made these recordings accessible to the public. There are a number of recordings related to the Chaney, Goodman, Schwerner case, capturing conversations between President Johnson and members of his administration, Congress, and members of the civil rights workers' families. These conversations are engrossing and bring the tensions related to the disappearance, search, and ultimate discovery of the three men vividly to life. One can listen to these recordings at http://millercenter.org/scripps/archive/presidentialrecordings/johnson. The Miller Center is also publishing annotated transcripts of these recordings. As of this writing, the most recently published volume of transcripts edited by Kent B. Germany and David C. Carter, *The Presidential Recordings: Lyndon B. Johnson: Mississippi Burning and the Passage of the Civil Rights Act, Volume Eight — June 23, 1964– July 4, 1964*, is a valuable research tool related to the Freedom Summer murders.

The 2005 trial of Edgar Ray Killen was televised, and this coverage can be found on C-SPAN at http://www.c-span.org.

I have relied heavily on newspaper accounts to tell this story, in particular the *New York Times*; the *Neshoba Democrat*; Jerry Mitchell's reporting in the *Clarion-Ledger* of Jackson, Mississippi; the *Yellow Springs [Ohio] News*, the *Los Angeles Times*; and the *Washington Post*. Magazine reporting was another valuable source of information, including *Life*, *Look*, *The New Yorker*, *People*, *US News & World Report*, and *Ramparts*.

Longtime Neshoba County, Mississippi, resident Florence Mars was an accomplished photographer, and her photo archive is located at the William F. Winter Archives and History Building in Jackson, Mississippi. A significant portion of the Mars archive comprises a rich portrayal of life in Neshoba County's black community.

The 2010 documentary film *Neshoba: The Price of Freedom*, by Micki Dickoff and Tony Pagano, chronicles the impact of the Chaney, Goodman, Schwerner murders on Neshoba County and the effort to bring Edgar Ray Killen to justice in 2005. This was another valuable source of background information, and a number of the individuals I interviewed for this book also appear in the documentary. Other films have been based on the Freedom Summer murders, including the 1975 two-part television docudrama *Attack on Terror: The FBI versus the Ku Klux Klan*, the 1988 film *Mississippi Burning*, and the 1990 television film *Murder in Mississippi*. The Freedom Summer murders have been addressed in other documentaries, including the documentary series *Eyes on the Prize*, part of which was nationally televised for the first time on PBS in 1987.

In 1964, the Department of Justice's code name for the disappearance and murder of the three civil rights workers was Mississippi Burning, or MIBURN for short. The MIBURN files comprise the FBI's investigative reports related to the case, and a select number of these documents, many of them redacted, can be found on the website http://vault.fbi.gov. The original files of the Mississippi Burning case, along with the full transcript of the 1967 federal trial, are stored at the National Archives, Southeast Region, in Morrow, Georgia. The documentary archive of Mississippi's now defunct spy agency, the Mississippi's Sovereignty Commission, can be found online at http://mdah.state.ms.us/arrec/digital _archives/sovcom. Miami University of Oxford, Ohio, has a History of Mississippi Freedom Summer Collection online at http://doyle .lib.muohio.edu/cdm4/browse.

There are a number of other websites that have been useful in researching this book. The Mississippi Historical Society can be found at http://mshistorynow.mdah.state.ms.us/mississippi-historical -society. The Mississippi Department of Archives and History in Jackson, Mississippi, can be found at http://mdah.state.ms.us. The Martin Luther King Jr. Center for Nonviolent Social Change in Atlanta, Georgia, is located at www.thekingcenter.org. The University of Southern Mississippi Center for Oral History and Cultural Heritage is located at http://www.usm.edu/history/oral -history, and the resources of the John F. Kennedy Presidential Library and Museum can be found at www.jfklibrary.org. For additional information about the Philadelphia Coalition, its website is http://www.neshobajustice.com.

As noted above, I am most indebted to the individuals who graciously consented to be interviewed and share experiences that were often difficult to revisit.

I would like to thank Ken Wright, who was an early and enthusiastic advocate for bringing this project to publication. I would also like to thank Michele Rubin and Susan Cohen of Writers House. Special thanks to my editor, Brenda Kosara, as well as the Scholastic staff, particularly Debra Dorfman, Marisa Polansky, Rachael Hicks, Jeannine Riske, and Marybeth Kavanagh.

Thanks also to Rosi Tominello, US Courts Librarian in Jackson, Mississippi, as well as the staff of the William F. Winter Archives and History Building in Jackson, Mississippi. I'm also grateful to Michal Schafer and Nancy Truehart for transcribing my interviews.

I would like to thank my wife, Grace, for her unfailing encouragement and support. I'm also grateful to my children, Logan Adlai and Ella Ruth — as always, crickets on my hearth — for their patience and understanding.

BIBLIOGRAPHY

Allen, James, Hilton Als, John Lewis, and Leon F. Litwack. *Without Sanctuary: Lynching Photography in America*. Santa Fe: Twin Palms Publishers, 2010.

Alston, Alex A., Jr., and James L. Dickerson. *Devil's Sanctuary: An Eyewitness History of Mississippi Hate Crimes*. Chicago: Lawrence Hill Books, 2009.

Andrews, Kenneth T. *Freedom Is a Constant Struggle: The Mississippi Civil Rights Movement and Its Legacy*. Chicago: The University of Chicago Press, 2004.

Asch, Chris Myers. *The Senator and the Sharecropper: The Freedom Struggles of James O. Eastland and Fannie Lou Hamer*. New York: The New Press, 2008.

Ball, Howard. *Murder in Mississippi: United States v. Price and the Struggle for Civil Rights*. Lawrence, KS: University Press of Kansas, 2004.

——. *Justice in Mississippi: The Murder Trial of Edgar Ray Killen*. Lawrence, KS: University Press of Kansas, 2006.

Bartoletti, Susan Campbell. *They Called Themselves the K.K.K.: The Birth of an American Terrorist Group*. New York: Houghton Mifflin Harcourt Publishing Company, 2010.

Belknap, Michal R. *Federal Law and Southern Order: Racial Violence and Constitutional Conflict in the Post-Brown South*. Athens, GA: The University of Georgia Press, 1995.

Bowers, Rick. *Spies of Mississippi: The True Story of the Spy Network That Tried to Destroy the Civil Rights Movement*.

With a foreword by Wade Henderson. Washington, DC: National Geographic, 2010.

Branch, Taylor. *Parting the Waters: America in the King Years 1954–63.* New York: Simon & Schuster, 1988.

——. *Pillar of Fire: America in the King Years 1963–65.* New York: Simon & Schuster, 1998.

——. *At Canaan's Edge: America in the King Years 1965–68.* New York: Simon & Schuster, 2006.

Burner, Eric R. *And Gently He Shall Lead Them: Robert Parris Moses and Civil Rights in Mississippi.* New York: New York University Press, 1994.

Busbee, Westley F., Jr. *Mississippi: A History.* Wheeling, IL: Harlan Davidson, Inc., 2005.

Cagin, Seth, and Philip Dray. *We Are Not Afraid: The Story of Goodman, Schwerner, and Chaney and the Civil Rights Campaign for Mississippi.* New York: MacMillan Publishing Company, 1988.

Cash, W. J. *The Mind of the South.* New York: Vintage Books, 1991.

Collins, Judy. *Sweet Judy Blue Eyes: My Life in Music.* New York: Crown Archetype, 2011.

Conroy, Pat. "Deacon Summer." In *Don't Quit Your Day Job: Acclaimed Authors and the Day Jobs They Quit,* edited by Sonny Brewer, 59–75. Douglas, Isle of Man: M. P. Publishing Limited, 2010.

Cox, Julian. *Road to Freedom: Photographs of the Civil Rights Movement, 1956–1968.* With an introduction by Charles Johnson. Atlanta: High Museum of Art, 2008.

Crosscup, Richard. *Children and Dramatics.* New York: Charles Scribner's Sons, 1966.

Dittmer, John. *Local People: The Struggle for Civil Rights in Mississippi.* Urbana and Chicago: University of Illinois Press, 1994.

Dray, Philip. *At the Hands of Persons Unknown: The Lynching of Black America*. New York: The Modern Library, 2002.

Durham, Michael S. *Powerful Days: The Civil Rights Photography of Charles Moore*. With an introduction by Andrew Young. Tuscaloosa, AL: The University of Alabama Press, 1991.

Emery, Kathy, Linda Reid Gold, and Sylvia Braselmann. *Lessons from Freedom Summer: Ordinary People Building Extraordinary Movements*. With a foreword by Howard Zinn. Monroe, ME: Common Courage Press, 2008.

Erenrich, Susie, ed. *Freedom Is a Constant Struggle: An Anthology of the Mississippi Civil Rights Movement*. Montgomery, AL: Black Belt Press, 1999.

Farmer, James. *Lay Bare the Heart: An Autobiography of the Civil Rights Movement*. With a foreword by Don Carleton. New York: Arbor House, 1985.

Faulkner, William. *William Faulkner: Essays, Speeches & Public Letters*. Edited by James B. Meriwether. New York: The Modern Library, 2004.

Germany, Kent B., and David C. Carter, eds. *The Presidential Recordings: Lyndon B. Johnson: Mississippi Burning and the Passage of the Civil Rights Act, Volume Eight — June 23, 1964–July 4, 1964*. New York: W. W. Norton & Company, 2011.

Hampton, Henry, Steve Fayer, with Sarah Flynn. *Voices of Freedom: An Oral History of the Civil Rights Movement from the 1950s Through the 1980s*. New York: Bantam Books, 1990.

Huie, William Bradford. *Three Lives for Mississippi*. With an introduction by Martin Luther King Jr. Jackson, MS: University Press of Mississippi, 2000. Originally published by WWC Books in 1965.

Irons, Jenny. *Reconstituting Whiteness: The Mississippi State Sovereignty Commission*. Nashville: Vanderbilt University Press, 2010.

Johnson, Jacqueline, ed. (Foreword by Keith Beauchamp) *Finding Freedom: Memorializing the Voices of Freedom Summer.* Oxford, Ohio: Miami University Press, 2013.

Kasher, Steven. *The Civil Rights Movement: A Photographic History, 1954–68.* With a foreword by Myrlie Evers-Williams. New York: Abbeville Press, 1996.

Katagiri, Yasuhiro. *The Mississippi State Sovereignty Commission: Civil Rights and States' Rights.* Jackson, MS: University Press of Mississippi, 2001.

Kunstler, William. M., with Sheila Isenberg. *My Life as a Radical Lawyer.* New York: Carol Publishing Group, 1994.

Levine, Ellen. *Freedom's Children: Young Civil Rights Activists Tell Their Own Stories.* New York: Puffin Books, 1993.

Lewis, John, with Michael D'Orso. *Walking with the Wind: A Memoir of the Movement.* New York: Simon & Schuster, 1998.

Lyon, Danny. *Memories of the Southern Civil Rights Movement.* With a foreword by Julian Bond. Santa Fe: Twin Palms Publishers, 2010.

Mars, Florence, with the assistance of Lynn Eden. *Witness in Philadelphia.* With a foreword by Turner Catledge. Baton Rouge: Louisiana State University Press, 1977.

Martinez, Elizabeth, ed. *Letters from Mississippi: Reports from Civil Rights Volunteers & Poetry of the 1964 Freedom Summer.* With an introduction by Julian Bond. Brookline, MA: Zephyr Press, 2007.

McMillen, Neil R. *The Citizens' Council: Organized Resistance to the Second Reconstruction, 1954–64.* Urbana and Chicago: University of Illinois Press, 1994.

——. *Dark Journey: Black Mississippians in the Age of Jim Crow.* Urbana and Chicago: University of Illinois Press, 1989.

McWhorter, Diane. *A Dream of Freedom: The Civil Rights Movement from 1954 to 1968.* With a foreword by Reverend Fred Shuttlesworth. New York: Scholastic Inc., 2004.

Mills, Kay. *This Little Light of Mine: The Life of Fannie Lou Hamer.* New York: Dutton, 1993.

Mills, Nicolaus. *Like a Holy Crusade: Mississippi 1964 — The Turning of the Civil Rights Movement in America.* Chicago: Ivan R. Dee, Inc., 1992.

Minor, Bill. *Eyes on Mississippi: A Fifty-Year Chronicle of Change.* Jackson, MS: J Richard Morris Books, 2001.

Mississippi Black Paper: Fifty-seven Negro and White Citizens' Testimony of Police Brutality, the Breakdown of Law and Order and the Corruption of Justice in Mississippi. With a foreword by Reinhold Niebuhr and an introduction by Hodding Carter III. New York: Random House, 1965.

Moody, Anne. *Coming of Age in Mississippi.* New York: Bantam Dell, 1968.

Moses, Robert P., and Charles E. Cobb Jr. *Radical Equations: Civil Rights from Mississippi to the Algebra Project.* Boston: Beacon Press, 2001.

Oshinsky, David M. *"Worse Than Slavery": Parchman Farm and the Ordeal of Jim Crow Justice.* New York: Free Press Paperbacks, 1996.

Payne, Charles M. *I've Got the Light of Freedom: The Organizing Tradition and the Mississippi Freedom Struggle.* Berkeley and Los Angeles: University of California Press, 2007.

Ransby, Barbara. *Ella Baker and the Black Freedom Movement: A Radical Democratic Vision.* Chapel Hill, NC: The University of North Carolina Press, 2003.

Reporting Civil Rights: Part One: American Journalism 1941–1963. New York: The Library of America, 2003.

Reporting Civil Rights: Part Two: American Journalism 1963–1973. New York: The Library of America, 2003.

Roberts, Gene, and Hank Klibanoff. *The Race Beat: The Press, the Civil Rights Struggle, and the Awakening of a Nation*. New York: Alfred A. Knopf, 2007.

Rosenberg, Jonathan, and Zachary Karabell. *Kennedy, Johnson, and the Quest for Justice: The Civil Rights Tapes*. New York: W. W. Norton & Company, 2003.

Schlesinger, Arthur M., Jr. *Robert Kennedy and His Times*. Boston: Houghton Mifflin Company, 1978.

Silver, James W. *Mississippi: The Closed Society*. New York: Harcourt, Brace & World, Inc., 1964.

———. *Running Scared: Silver in Mississippi*. Jackson: University Press of Mississippi, 1984.

Smith, Kenneth L., and Ira G. Zepp Jr. *Search for the Beloved Community: The Thinking of Martin Luther King, Jr.* With a foreword by Lewis V. Baldwin. Valley Forge, PA: Judson Press, 1998.

Sugarman, Tracy. *We Had Sneakers, They Had Guns: The Kids Who Fought for Civil Rights in Mississippi*. Syracuse, NY: Syracuse University Press, 2009.

Sutherland, Elizabeth, ed. *Letters from Mississippi*. With an introduction by Julian Bond. New York: McGraw-Hill Book Company, 1965.

Tusa, Bobs M. *Faces of Freedom Summer*. Photographs by Herbert Randall. With a foreword by Victoria Jackson Gray Adams and Cecil Gray. Tuscaloosa: The University of Alabama Press, 2001.

Watson, Bruce. *Freedom Summer: The Savage Season That Made Mississippi Burn and Made America a Democracy*. New York: Viking, 2010.

Weiner, Tim. *Enemies: A History of the FBI.* New York: Random House, 2012.

Williams, Juan. *Eyes on the Prize: America's Civil Rights Years, 1954–1965.* With an introduction by Julian Bond. New York: Viking, 1987.

Winstead, Mary. *Back to Mississippi: A Personal Journey Through the Events that Changed America in 1964.* New York: Hyperion, 2002.

INDEX

Page references in *italics* indicate material in illustrations or photographs.